Fodor's New
FIRST EDITION

Pocket Rome

KU-521-343

Reprinted from *Fodor's Italy*

Fodor's Travel Publications, Inc.
New York • Toronto • London •
Sydney • Auckland

First Edition

ISBN 0–679–02754–8

Thanks to Methuen, London, for permission to reprint from H. V. Morton's *A Traveller in Rome* (1957).

Fodor's Pocket Rome

Editor: Hannah Borgeson
Contributors: Barbara Walsh Angelillo, Robert Blake, Echo Garrett, Bevin McLaughlin, Mary Ellen Schultz, Nancy van Itallie
Creative Director: Fabrizio La Rocca
Cartographer: David Lindroth
Illustrator: Karl Tanner
Cover Photograph: Mauro Sorani/Vision
Design: Vignelli Associates

Special Sales

Contents

Maps

Foreword

While every care has been taken to ensure the accuracy of the information in this guide, the passage of time will always bring change, and consequently, the publisher cannot accept responsibility for errors that may occur.

All prices and opening times quoted here are based on information supplied to us at press time. Hours and admission fees may change, however, and the prudent traveler will avoid inconvenience by calling ahead.

Fodor's wants to hear about your travel experiences, both pleasant and unpleasant. When a hotel or restaurant fails to live up to its billing, let us know and we will investigate the complaint and revise our entries where the facts warrant it.

Send your letters to the editors of Fodor's Travel Publications, 201 East 50th Street, New York, NY 10022.

Rome

Introduction

By Leslie Gardiner

A freelance writer and broadcaster, Leslie Gardiner has known Italy since 1942 when, as an escaped prisoner of war, he walked from the Alps to Sicily, a journey he has repeated on foot and by road and rail many times since.

Coming off the autostrada at Fiano Romano or Roma Sud exit, you know by the convergence of heavily trafficked routes that you are entering a grand nexus: All roads lead to Rome. And then the interminable suburbs, the railroad crossings, the intersections—no wonder they call it the Eternal City.

Nearer the center, Rome begins to have the air of a city socially divided. On one side, compact masses of old tenements crowd above mean streets. On the other, soaring yellow-washed apartment blocks, five stories high with inner courtyards, are geometrically aligned. Poor or not-so-poor, your Roman likes living in a crowd, in the thick of things. The residential suburb, out at Monte Sacro or Garbatella, has little appeal for him.

In the urban sprawl a few features that match your expectations of Rome begin to take shape: a bridge with heroic statues along its parapets; a towering cake of frothy marble decorated with allegorical figures in extravagant poses; a piazza and an obelisk under an umbrella of pine trees; a fountain pitted with age, bearing the notice *ACQUA NON POTABILE*—which doesn't prevent street urchins from dashing up to drink at it. Street names touch a chord of schoolroom memories: Via Appia Nuova, Via Aurelia Antica. The very gratings and manhole covers are stamped SPQR, "The Senate and Populace of Rome," an expression that links the citizen with his ancestor of 22 centuries ago and gives the stranger the eerie feeling that the dust he stirs has been stirred by the togas of Cato, Cicero, and Seneca. In Rome, 22 centuries are just a few generations back.

You have arrived. You are in the city's heart. Your automobile is parked in the shadow of a stone she-wolf, along with automobiles which have ROMA on their license plates. Italian index letters are abbreviations of the vehicle-licensing towns, MI for Milan, GE for Genoa and so on—except in Rome. The Roman motorist wears ROMA, spelled out in full. Like the SPQR, that was Mussolini's doing. He reasserted the grandeur that was ROME. He made Romans understand that they were the children of heroes and demigods.

U p north, they tell us that Turin with its industry and Milan with its commerce are the true capital cities of Italy. Rome is badly planned, badly sited, too far south, too enervating in summer, a town of lawyers, civil servants, and tourists. But the Romans can smile at that. They know they inhabit the fountainhead of the Western world, not solely of Italy. They know that their town, and no other, collected the wisdom of Egypt and Greece, refined and enriched it, and supplied the nations which arose afterward with their laws, systems of government, religions, military arts, and the foundations of their language and literature. Those black-eyed urchins at the wall-fountain, that gross woman bawling from her tiny balcony, that grandfather snoring on a cane chair at street level, that white-robed child emerging from the side door of the church, that pallid waiter polishing the restaurant window with yesterday's newspaper—all can say, as their distant ancestors said, *Civis Romanus sum*—"I am a Roman citizen." If they should travel to other parts of Italy they will note without surprise that most main streets are called Via Roma; that every medieval walled town has its Porta Romana, the gate that faces Rome; and that, on posts beside every main road, the distance to Rome is recorded every tenth of a kilometer.

Rome was not built in a day, though much of superficial Rome was built in less than a century. The old city grew organically, and still grows, and its growth is chronicled in its stones. When you look into this city you see how, like Troy, it exists on several levels. Unlike the levels of Troy, these have each been a spiritual metropolis for whole societies of human beings, most of whom never set eyes on Rome. Under the swarming traffic lie traces of Etruscan Rome; ancient Veii and Caere, strongholds of Etruscan princes, are virtually part of modern Rome.

There is a Rome of the Republics and the Emperors, outcropping in unexpected places like barbershops, garage forecourts, and railroad sidings. There is an early Christian Rome, tunneling away in the catacombs, and a Dark Age Rome, when the pampered citizenry fled to Carthage and, on arrival, immediately wanted to know what was playing at the theater. Engineers working on sewers or boring for extensions to the metropolitana (the subway) run afoul of the relics. A constant war is waged between archaeology departments and the town planners.

There are gaps in history's stratification. In the Middle Ages the city was reduced to a rural slum on the banks of an evil-smelling Tiber, and the malarial heirs of imperial grandeur borrowed classical pillars to repair their hovels. There is also Rome of the papacies, and Rome of a period when the popes were hunted in and out like criminals. There is evidence of Byzantine Rome, of the dark little brick-and-tile churches that incorporated Rome's name in an architectural style (Romanesque), and of the sumptuous flowering of the later Renaissance styles which are called Roman Baroque.

Rome, however, though rich in florid sculptures, intricate ornamental motifs, and neoclassical effects, cannot show us galleries of famous paintings the way many provincial centers can. For a capital city, it lacks a capital display of national artists. The Italian heritage is spread over the whole country; all major cities and many small towns and villages have their share of the treasure.

Closer to the present day and to the surface of Rome lies the early 19th-century city, destination of Grand Tourists. That is the Rome of Gioacchino Belli, dialect poet and satirist, and of Goethe's and Stendhal's travel books. In the English quarter, at the foot of the Spanish Steps, the poet John Keats died and Mrs. Babington kept her teashop.

Students of the Risorgimento—the resurgence and reunification of Italy in the 19th century—know a Rome of Garibaldi and his insurgents. From a vantage point on the Janiculum, the hero on horseback surveys the terrain in bloody skirmishes and betrayals. Pigeons from St. Peter's Square love to fly up and perch on the saddle of that equestrian statue, so that it often looks as though Garibaldi is carrying the birds to market.

Toward the end of the last century, the Eternal City spread its wings. On September 20, 1870 (Via Venti Settembre is one of the most durable of Italian street names), General Cadorna's regiment of *bersaglieri* breached the Porta Pia, proclaimed Rome capital of Italy, and made Pope Pius IX the "prisoner of the Vatican." The gold rush of merchants and contractors from the north, the arrival of hordes of bureaucrats from Florence, briefly the former capital, and of poor immigrants from Naples and Calabria, doubled the population of 100,000 in days, and took it to half a million in months. The Via Nazionale and the Via Venti Settembre were christened and the city-center slums were cleared for public buildings more in keeping with Rome's dignity. But the new city council rejected Garibaldi's scheme for diverting the Tiber. Without the Tiber, floods and all, Rome would not have been Rome.

Much of modern Rome, therefore, went up in a few years in the 1880s, decade of the *gran febbre di Roma* ("great fever of Rome")—a fever that ended with the patient's total collapse. "Through greed and childish dreams," a newspaper said, "the bankers have promoted building in a manner devoid of all prudence . . . . Every stage of construction depended on promissory notes. . . . When foreign bankers refused to discount notes, the paper tower crumbled."

The so-called "building yard of Italy" in the later 1880s was a field of ruins among the classical ruins, infested by provincials whom the promise of work had drawn in by the thousand. Rome grew dirtier and more decrepit, littered with shacks and cardboard tents until well into the present century. Of the 1920 population of 800,000, it was reported that nearly one fifth of all citizens lived in "abusive dwellings." Then came Fascism, which ruthlessly swept them away. Wreckers moved into Trastevere and the slums near the Capitol, homes of those who could most truly claim Roman citizenship. A new central thoroughfare, the broad Via dei Fori Imperiali, was laid down from Mussolini's Palazzo Venezia to the Colosseum of the Caesars. One human touch was the rebuilding of the old *rione* (district) fountains, the sculpted wells of the different parishes—an important feature of tourist Rome today.

Monumental architecture of the past 50 years has not much disturbed the shabby but stylish buildings of central Rome. No skyscraper outtops the 450-foot dome of St. Peter's. New-look architecture, by exponents of the school of Gio Ponti and Nervi, is almost wholly confined to the EUR complex, site of the aborted Universal Exposition of Rome in 1942 and Olympic venue of 1960—a suburb bigger than Florence. On the whole, modern buildings look pretentious and ephemeral, and they fall far short of tradition. Through the '50s and the '60s there was an uncontrolled expansion of building along the main exit roads, but this has now long since been checked and many who can't find reasonably priced housing in Rome have moved to satellite towns in the Alban and Sabine hills. Rome has once again its Gypsy encampments among the arches of the old aqueducts, especially on the eastern approaches, Via Casilina and the Cinecittà area. But it is decreed that the city itself—beautiful and pleasing in spite of everything—shall be confined within its present limits.

1 Essential Information

Before You Go

Government Tourist Offices

In the United States Contact the Italian Government Travel Office at 630 5th Avenue, Suite 1565, New York, NY 10111, tel. 212/245–4822, fax 212/586–9249; 500 North Michigan Avenue, Chicago, IL 60611, tel. 312/644–0990, fax 312/644–3019; 12400 Wilshire Boulevard, Suite 550, Los Angeles, CA 90025, tel. 310/820–0098, fax 310/820–6357.

In Canada 1 Place Ville Marie, Montreal, Quebec H3B 3M9, tel. 514/866–7667.

In the United Kingdom 1 Princes Street, London W1R 8AY England, tel. 0171/408–1254.

When to Go

Rome's main tourist season runs from mid-April to the end of September. Foreign tourists crowd the city at Easter, when Italians flock to resorts and to the country. From March through May, bus loads of eager schoolchildren on excursions take Rome by storm. The best months for sightseeing are April, May, June, September, and October, when the weather is generally pleasant and not too hot. The hottest months are July and August, when brief afternoon thunderstorms are common. Winters are relatively mild but always include some rainy spells.

If you can avoid it, don't travel at all in Italy in August, when much of the population is on the move. The heat can be oppressive, and vacationing Italians cram roads, trains, and planes on their way to shore and mountain resorts. All this is especially true around Ferragosto, the August 15 national holiday, when Rome is deserted and many restaurants and shops are closed.

Rome has no official off-season as far as hotel rates go, though some hotels will reduce rates during the slack season upon request. Always inquire about special rates.

Climate The following are average daily maximum and minimum temperatures for Rome.

Jan.	52F	11C	May	74F	23C	Sept.	79F	26C
	40	5		56	13		62	17
Feb.	55F	13C	June	82F	28C	Oct.	71F	22C
	42	6		63	17		55	13
Mar.	59F	15C	July	87F	30C	Nov.	61F	16C
	45	7		67	20		49	10
Apr.	66F	19C	Aug.	86F	30C	Dec.	55F	13C
	50	10		67	20		44	6

Information Sources For current weather conditions and forecasts for cities in the United States and abroad, plus the local time and helpful travel tips, call the **Weather Channel Connection** (tel. 900/932–8437; 95¢ per minute) from a touch-tone phone.

National Holidays January 1 (New Year's Day); January 6 (Epiphany); April 16, 17 (Easter Sunday and Monday); April 25 (Liberation Day); May 1 (Labor Day or May Day); August 15 (Assumption of Mary, also known as Ferragosto); November 1 (All Saints Day); December 8 (Immaculate Conception); December 25, 26 (Christmas Day and Boxing Day).

The feast days of patron saints are also holidays, observed locally. Many businesses and shops may be closed in Rome on June 29 (Sts. Peter and Paul).

What to Pack

Clothing The weather is considerably milder in Rome all year round than it is in the north and central United States or Great Britain. In summer, stick with clothing that's as light as possible, although a sweater or woolen stole may be necessary in the evening, even during the hot months. Brief summer afternoon thunderstorms are common, so carry a folding umbrella. During the winter a medium-weight coat and a raincoat will stand you in good stead. Central heating may not be up to your standards and interiors can be cold and damp; take wools rather than sheer fabrics, flannel rather than flimsy nightwear, and boots or shoes that can accommodate socks rather than dainty pumps. Pack sturdy walking shoes, preferably with crepe or rubber soles, at any time of the year, because cobblestone streets and gravel paths are common and can be murder on feet and footwear.

In general, Italians dress well and are not sloppy. They do not usually wear shorts in the city, unless longish bermudas happen to be in fashion. Even when dressed casually or informally, they are careful about the way they look, which is why so few restaurants establish dress codes. Men aren't required to wear ties or jackets anywhere, except in some of the grander hotel dining rooms and top-level restaurants. Formal wear is the exception rather than the rule at the opera nowadays, though people in expensive seats usually do get dressed up.

Dress codes are strict for visits to churches—especially St. Peter's—and to the Vatican Museums. Women must cover bare shoulders and arms—a shawl will do—but no longer need cover their heads. Shorts are taboo for men and women. For the huge general papal audiences, no rules of dress apply other than those of common sense. For other types of audience, the Vatican Information Office will give requirements.

Miscellaneous To protect yourself against purse snatchers and pickpockets, take a handbag with long straps that you can sling across your body bandolier-style and with a zippered compartment for your money and other valuables. Better yet, wear a money belt. Take your own soap if you stay in budget hotels: Many do not provide soap or give guests only one tiny bar per room. Also, travel with a wash cloth, or face flannel, if you use one; Italian hotels generally supply only towels. Bring an extra pair of eyeglasses or contact lenses in your carry-on luggage. If you have a health problem that requires a prescription drug, pack enough to last the duration of the trip or have your doctor write a prescription using the drug's generic name, because brand names vary from country to country. Always carry prescription drugs in their original packaging to avoid problems with customs officials. Don't pack them in luggage that you plan to check, in case your bags go astray. Pack a list of the offices that supply refunds for lost or stolen traveler's checks.

Electricity The electrical current is 220 volts, 50 cycles alternating current (AC); the United States runs on 110-volt, 60-cycle AC current. Unlike wall outlets in the United States, which accept plugs that have two flat prongs, Italian outlets take Continental-type plugs, with two round prongs.

Adapters, To use U.S.-made electric appliances abroad,
Converters, you'll need an adapter plug. Unless the appli-
Transformers ance is dual-voltage and made for travel, you'll also need a converter. Hotels sometimes have 110-volt outlets for low-wattage appliances (marked "For Shavers Only") near the sink; don't use them for a high-wattage appliance like a blowdryer. If you're traveling with an older laptop computer, carry a transformer. New laptop computers are auto-sensing, operating equally well on 110 and 220 volts, so you need only the appropriate adapter plug.

Luggage Free airline baggage allowances depend on the
Regulations airline, the route, and the class of your ticket; ask in advance. In general, on domestic flights and on flights between the United States and foreign destinations, you are entitled to check two bags—neither exceeding 62 inches, or 158 centimeters (length + width + height), or weighing more than 70 pounds (32 kilograms). A third piece may be brought aboard as a carryon; its total dimensions are generally limited to less than 45 inches (114 centimeters), so it will fit under the seat in front of you or in the overhead compartment. In the United States, the Federal Aviation Administration gives airlines broad latitude to limit carry-on allowances and tailor them to different aircraft and operational conditions. Charges for excess, oversize, or overweight pieces vary, so inquire before you pack.

If you are flying between two foreign destinations, note that baggage allowances may be determined not by the piece method but by the weight method, which generally allows 88 pounds (40 kilograms) of luggage in first class, 66 pounds (30 kilograms) in business class, and 44 pounds (20 kilograms) in economy. If your flight between two cities abroad *connects* with your transatlantic flight, the piece method still applies.

Safeguarding Before leaving home, itemize your bags' con-
Your Luggage tents and their worth in case they go astray. To minimize that risk, tag them inside and out with your name, address, and phone number. (If you

use your home address, cover it so that potential thieves can't see it.) Put a copy of your itinerary inside each bag, so that you can easily be tracked. At check-in, make sure that the tag attached by baggage handlers bears the correct three-letter code for your destination. If your bags do not arrive with you, or if you detect damage, immediately file a written report with the airline before you leave the airport.

Italian Currency

The unit of currency in Italy is the lira, plural lire. There are bills of 100,000, 10,000, 5,000, 2,000, and 1,000 lire. Coins are 500, 200, 100, 50, 20, and 10, but the last two are rarely found, and prices are often rounded out to the nearest 50 lire. At press time (August 1994) the exchange rate was about 1,550 lire to the U.S. dollar, 1,157 lire to the Canadian dollar, and 2,402 lire to the pound sterling.

Passports and Visas

If your passport is lost or stolen abroad, report the loss immediately to the nearest embassy or consulate and to the local police. If you can provide the consular officer with the information contained in the passport, he or she will usually be able to issue you a new passport promptly. For this reason, keep a photocopy of the data page of your passport separate from your money and traveler's checks. Also leave a photocopy with a relative or friend at home.

U.S. Citizens All U.S. citizens, even infants, need a valid passport to enter Italy for stays of up to three months. You can pick up new and renewal application forms at any of the 13 U.S. Passport Agency offices and at some post offices and courthouses. Although passports are usually mailed within four weeks of your application's receipt, allow five weeks or more from April through summer. Call the Department of State Office of Passport Services' information line (tel. 202/647–0518) for fees, documentation requirements, and other details.

Canadian Citizens Canadian citizens need a valid passport to enter Italy for stays of up to three months; check with the Italian consulate regarding longer stays.

Regional passport offices, post offices, and travel agencies have application forms. Whether for a first or subsequent passport, you must apply in person. Children under 16 may be included on a parent's passport but must have their own to travel alone. Passports are valid for five years and are usually mailed within two weeks of an application's receipt. For information in English or French, call the passport office (tel. 514/283–2152 or 800/567–6868).

U.K. Citizens Citizens of the United Kingdom need a valid passport to enter Italy for purposes of tourism. Applications for new and renewal passports are available from main post offices as well as at the six passport offices, located in Belfast, Glasgow, Liverpool, London, Newport, and Peterborough. You may apply in person at all passport offices, or by mail to all except the London office. Children under 16 may travel on an accompanying parent's passport. All passports are valid for 10 years. Allow a month for processing.

A British Visitor's Passport is valid for holidays and some business trips of up to three months to Italy. It can include both partners of a married couple. Valid for one year, it will be issued on the same day that you apply. You must apply in person at a main post office.

Customs and Duties

On Arrival There are two levels of duty-free allowances for visitors to Italy.

For goods from outside the European Union or for goods purchased in a duty-free shop in an EU country, the allowances are: (1) 200 cigarettes or 100 cigarillos or 50 cigars or 250 grams of tobacco; (2) 2 liters of still table wine plus (3) 1 liter of spirits over 22% volume or 2 liters of spirits under 22% volume (fortified and sparkling wines); and (4) 60 milliliters of perfume and 250 milliliters of toilet water.

For goods obtained (duty and tax paid) within another EU country, the allowances are: (1) 300 cigarettes or 150 cigarillos or 75 cigars or 400 grams of tobacco; (2) 5 liters of still table wine plus (3) 1.5 liters of spirits over 22% volume or 5 liters of spirits under 22% volume (fortified or sparkling wines) or 3 more liters of table wine; and (4) 75 milliliters of perfume and 375 milliliters of toilet water.

Other items including cameras and films can be brought in duty-free up to a value of £136 for non-EU citizens, £71 for EU citizens. Officially, two still cameras with 10 rolls of film each and one movie camera with 10 rolls of film may be brought in duty-free. Other items intended for personal use are generally admitted, as long as the quantities are reasonable.

Returning Home
U.S. Customs
If you've been out of the United States for at least 48 hours and haven't already used any part of the exemption in the past 30 days, you may bring home $400 worth of foreign goods duty-free. So can each member of your family, and your exemptions may be pooled so that one of you can bring in more if another brings in less. A 10% duty applies to the next $1,000 of goods; above $1,400, the rate varies with the merchandise. (If the 48-hour or 30-day limits apply, your duty-free allowance drops to $25, which may *not* be pooled.)

Travelers 21 or older may bring back one liter of alcohol duty-free, provided the beverage laws of the state through which they reenter the U.S. allow it. In addition, 100 non-Cuban cigars and 200 cigarettes are allowed, regardless of age. Antiques and works of art over 100 years old are duty-free.

Gifts valued at less than $50 may be mailed to the United States duty-free, with a limit of one package per day per addressee, and do not count as part of your exemption (do not send alcohol or tobacco products or perfume valued at more than $5); mark the package "Unsolicited Gift" and write the nature of the gift and its retail value on the outside. Most reputable stores will handle the mailing for you.

For a copy of "Know Before You Go," a free brochure detailing what you may and may not bring back to the United States, rates of duty, and other pointers, contact the **U.S. Customs Service** (Box 7407, Washington, DC 20044, tel. 202/927-6724).

Canadian Once per calendar year, when you've been out of
Customs Canada for at least seven days, you may bring in
C$300 worth of goods duty-free. If you've been
away less than seven days but more than 48
hours, the duty-free exemption drops to C$100
but can be claimed any number of times (as can a
C$20 duty-free exemption for absences of 24
hours or more). You cannot combine the yearly
and 48-hour exemptions, use the C$300 exemp-
tion only partially (to save the balance for a later
trip), or pool exemptions with family members.
Goods claimed under the C$300 exemption may
follow you by mail; those claimed under the less-
er exemptions must accompany you.

Alcohol and tobacco products may be included in
the yearly and 48-hour exemptions but not in the
24-hour exemption, and they must accompany
you. If you meet the age requirements of the
province through which you reenter Canada,
you may bring in, duty-free, 1.14 liters (40 imperial ounces) of wine or liquor *or* two dozen 12-
ounce cans or bottles of beer or ale. If you are 16
or older, you may bring in, duty-free, 200 cigarettes, 50 cigars or cigarillos, and 400 tobacco
sticks or 400 grams of manufactured tobacco.

An unlimited number of gifts valued up to C$60
each may be mailed to Canada duty-free. These
do not count as part of your exemption. Label
the package "Unsolicited Gift—Value under
$60." Alcohol and tobacco are excluded.

For more information, ask the Revenue Canada
Customs and Excise Department (2265 St.
Laurent Blvd. S, Ottawa, Ontario K1G 4K3, tel.
613/957–0275) for a copy of the free brochure "I
Declare/Je Déclare."

U.K. Customs If your journey was wholly within EU countries, you no longer need to pass through customs when you return to the United Kingdom.
According to EU guidelines, you may bring in
800 cigarettes, 400 cigarillos, 200 cigars, and 1
kilogram of smoking tobacco, plus 10 liters of
spirits, 20 liters of fortified wine, 90 liters of
wine, and 110 liters of beer. If you exceed these
limits, you may be required to prove that the
goods are for your personal use or are gifts.

No animals or pets can be brought into the United Kingdom without a lengthy quarantine. The law is strictly enforced with severe penalties.

For further information or a copy of "A Guide for Travellers," which details standard customs procedures as well as what you may bring into the United Kingdom from abroad, contact HM Customs and Excise (Dorset House, Stamford St., London SE1 9PY, tel. 0171/928–3344).

Language

In Rome, language is no problem. You can always find someone who speaks a little English, albeit with a heavy accent; remember that the Italian language is pronounced exactly as it is written (many Italians try to speak English as it is written, with disconcerting results).

The exhortation "Va via!" (Go away!) is useful in warding off beggars.

Arriving and Departing

From North America by Plane

Flights are either nonstop, direct, or connecting. A nonstop flight requires no change of plane and makes no stops. A direct flight stops at least once and can involve a change of plane, although the flight number remains the same; if the first leg is late, the second waits. This is not the case with a connecting flight, which involves a different plane and a different flight number.

Airports and Airlines Airlines serving Rome nonstop from the United States are **Alitalia** (tel. 800/223–5730), **Delta** (tel. 800/241–4141), and **TWA** (tel. 800/892–4141). These flights land at Rome's **Leonardo da Vinci Airport,** better known as Fiumicino. Some international charter flights land at **Ciampino,** a military airport on the Via Appia Nuova, 15 kilometers (9 miles) from the center of Rome.

Flying Time The flying time to Rome from New York is 8½ hours; from Chicago, 10–11 hours; from Los Angeles, 12–13 hours.

Between Leonardo da Vinci Airport and Downtown By Train To get to downtown Rome from Fiumicino airport you have a choice of two trains. Inquire at the airport (at EPT or train information counters) as to which takes you closest to your hotel. The non-stop Airport-Termini express takes you directly to Track 22 at Termini station, Rome's main train station, well served by taxis and the hub of Metro and bus lines. The ride to Termini takes 30 minutes; departures are hourly, beginning at 7:50 AM from the airport, with a final departure at 10:55 PM. Tickets cost 12,000 lire. The other airport train has its terminal at Tiburtina train station, east of downtown Rome. It makes several stops, including Trastevere and Ostiense stations, on the southern fringes of downtown Rome. This train departs every 20 minutes from 6 AM to 10 PM. The ride to Tiburtina takes 40 minutes. Tickets cost 7,000 lire. For either train you buy your ticket at automatic vending machines. There are ticket counters at some stations (Termini Track 22, Trastevere, Tiburtina).

By Taxi A taxi from the airport to the center of town costs about 60,000 lire, including supplements for airport service and luggage, and the ride takes 30–40 minutes, depending on traffic. Private limousines can be hired at booths in the arrivals hall; they charge a little more than taxis but can take more passengers. Ignore gypsy drivers; stick to yellow or white cabs. A booth in the arrivals hall provides taxi information.

By Car Follow the signs for Rome on the expressway, which links with the Grande Raccordo Anulare (GRA), the beltway around Rome. The direction you take on the GRA depends on where your hotel is, so get directions from the car-rental people at the airport.

From the United Kingdom by Plane

Alitalia (tel. 0171/602–7111) and **British Airways** (tel. 0181/897–4000) operate direct flights from London (Heathrow) to Rome. Flying time is 2½ to three hours. There's also one direct flight a week from Manchester to Rome. Standard fares are extremely high. Both airlines offer less expensive APEX tickets (usual booking restrictions apply) and PEX and Super-PEX tickets (which don't have to be bought in advance). The Eurobudget ticket (no length-of-stay or advance-purchase restrictions) is another option.

By Car, Train, and Bus

By Car The main access routes from the north are A1 (Autostrada del Sole) from Milan and Florence or the A12/E80 highway from Genoa. The principal route to or from points south, including Naples, is the A2. All highways connect with the GRA, which channels traffic into the center. Markings on the GRA are confusing: Take time to study the route you need.

By Train Termini Station is Rome's main train terminal; the Tiburtina and Ostiense stations serve a few long-distance trains. Some trains for Pisa and Genoa leave Rome from, or pass through, the Trastevere Station. For train information, call tel. 06/4775, 7 AM–10:40 PM. You can find English-speaking staff at the information office at Termini Station, or ask for information at travel agencies. If you purchase tickets and book seat reservations in advance either at the main stations or at travel agencies bearing the FS (Ferrovie dello Stato) emblem, you'll avoid long lines at ticket windows. Additionally, ticket windows on the lower concourse in Termini Station sell tickets and reserve seats for all trains, and also sell subway, bus, and airport train tickets. Tickets for train rides within a radius of 100 kilometers of Rome can be purchased at tobacco shops as well as at ticket machines on the main concourse.

By Bus Rome has no central bus terminal; long-distance and suburban buses terminate either near Termini Station or near Metro stops. COTRAL is the bus company that connects Rome with outlying areas and other cities in the Lazio region. For COTRAL bus information, call tel. 06/591–5551, Mon.–Fri. 7 AM–6 , Sat. 7 AM–2 PM.

Staying in Rome

Important Addresses and Numbers

Tourist Information The main **EPT** (Rome Provincial Tourist Office) is at Via Parigi 5, tel. 06/488–3748. Open Mon.–Fri. 8:15–7:15, Sat. 8:15–1:15. There are also

EPT booths at Termini Station and Leonardo da Vinci airport.

Consulates **U.S. Consulate** (Via Veneto 121, tel. 06/46741). **Canadian Consulate** (Via Zara 30, tel. 06/440–3028). **U.K. Consulate** (Via Venti Settembre 80A, tel. 06/482–5441).

Emergencies **Police,** tel. 06/4686.

Ambulance (Red Cross), tel. 06/5100.

Doctors and Dentists: Call your consulate or the private Salvator Mundi Hospital (tel. 06/589–4867) or Rome American Hospital (tel. 06/22551), which have English-speaking staff, for recommendations.

Late-Night Pharmacies You will find American and British products—or their equivalents—and English-speaking staff at **Farmacia Internazionale Capranica** (Piazza Capranica 96, tel. 056/679–4680), **Farmacia Internazionale Barberini** (Piazza Barberini 49, tel. 06/482–5456), and **Farmacia Doricchi** (Via Venti Settembre 47, tel. 06/487–3880), among others. Most are open 8:30–1, 4–8; some are open all night. Pharmacies take turns opening on Sunday. Each pharmacy posts a schedule.

English-Language Bookstores English-language paperback books and magazines are available at newsstands in the center of Rome, especially on Via Veneto. For all types of books in English, visit the **Economy Book and Video Center** (Via Torino 136, tel. 06/474–6877), the **Anglo-American Bookstore** (Via della Vite 27, tel. 06/679–5222), or the **Lion Bookshop** (Via del Babuino 181, tel. 06/322–5837).

Travel Agencies **American Express** (Piazza di Spagna 38, tel. 06/67641), **CIT** (Piazza della Repubblica 64, tel. 06/47941), **Wagons Lits** (Via Boncompagni 25, tel. 06/481–7655).

Telephones

Local Calls Pay phones take either a 200-lire coin, two 100-lire coins, a *gettone* (token), or a *scheda* (prepaid calling card). The gettone-only phones are being phased out; if you happen upon one, buy tokens from the nearest cashier or the token machine near the phone. Insert the token (which doesn't drop right away), dial your number, wait for an answer, then complete the connection by pushing the knob at the token slot. When the token drops, the other party is able to hear you. Scheda phones are becoming common everywhere. You buy the card (values vary) at Telefoni offices and tobacconists. Insert the card as indicated by the arrow, and its value will be visible in the window. After you hang up, the card is returned so you can use it until its value runs out. The card makes long-distance direct dialing (*teleselezione*) much easier—without it, insert at least five coins and have more handy; unused coins will be returned.

International Calls Since hotels tend to overcharge, sometimes exorbitantly, for long-distance and international calls, it is best to make such calls from Telefoni offices, where operators will assign you a booth, help you place your call, and collect payment when you have finished, at no extra charge. There are Telefoni offices, designated *SIP* (sometimes also *ASST*), in all cities and towns. You can make collect calls from any phone by dialing 170, which will get you an English-speaking operator. Rates to the United States are lowest round the clock on Sunday and 11 PM–8 AM, Italian time, on weekdays.

Operators and Information For general information in English on calling in Europe and the Mediterranean area, dial 176. For operator-assisted service in those areas, dial 15. For operator-assisted service and information regarding intercontinental calls, dial 170. The country code for Italy is 39; Rome's city code is 6.

Mail

Postal Rates Airmail letters to the United States and Canada cost 1,100 lire for the first 19 grams and an additional 1,700 lire for up to 50 grams. Airmail postcards cost 950 lire if the message is limited to a few words and a signature; otherwise, you pay the letter rate. Airmail letters to the United Kingdom cost 750 lire; postcards, 650 lire. You can buy stamps at tobacconists.

Receiving Mail Mail service is generally slow; allow up to 14 days for mail from Britain, 21 days from North

America. Correspondence can be addressed to you care of the Italian post office. Letters should be addressed to your name, "c/o Ufficio Postale Centrale," followed by "FERMO POSTA" on the next line, and the name of the city (preceded by its postal code) on the next. You can collect it at the central post office by showing your passport or photo-bearing ID and paying a small fee. American Express also has a general-delivery service. There's no charge for cardholders, holders of American Express Traveler's checks, or anyone who booked a vacation with American Express.

Tipping

The following guidelines apply in Rome; Italians tip smaller amounts in smaller cities and towns.

In restaurants a service charge of about 15% usually appears as a separate item on your check. A few restaurants state on the menu that cover and service charge are included. Either way, it's customary to leave an additional 5%–10% tip for the waiter, depending on the service. Checkroom attendants expect 500 lire per person. Restroom attendants are given from 200 lire in public restrooms, and more in expensive hotels and restaurants. Tip 100 lire for whatever you drink standing up at a coffee bar, 500 lire or more for table service in a smart café, and less in neighborhood cafés. At a hotel bar tip 1,000 lire for a round or two of cocktails.

Taxi drivers are usually happy with 5%–10% of the meter amount. Railway and airport porters charge a fixed rate per bag. Tip an additional 500 lire per person, but more if the porter is very helpful. Theater ushers expect 500 lire per person, but more for very expensive seats. Give a barber 2,000–3,000 lire and a hairdresser's assistant 3,000–8,000 lire for a shampoo or cut, depending on the type of establishment.

Tip guides about 2,000 lire per person for a half-day group sightseeing tour, more if they are very good. In museums and other places of interest where admission is free, an offering is expected; give anything from 500 to 1,000 lire for one or two persons, more if the guardian has been especially helpful. Service station attendants are tipped only for special services.

In hotels, give the *portière* about 15% of the bill for services, or 5,000–10,000 lire if he or she has been generally helpful. For two people in a double room, leave the chambermaid about 1,000 lire per day, or about 4,000–5,000 a week, in a moderate ($$) hotel (*see* Chapter 5, Dining, and Chapter 6, Lodging, for a definition of price categories); tip a minimum of 1,000 lire for valet or room service. Increase these amounts by one-half in an expensive ($$$) hotel, and double them in a very expensive ($$$$) hotel. Tip doormen in a very expensive hotel 1,000 lire for calling a cab and 2,000 lire for carrying bags to the check-in desk. In a very expensive hotel tip a bellhop 2,000–5,000 lire for carrying your bags to the room and 2,000–3,000 lire for room service. In a moderate hotel tip a bellhop 1,000–2,000 lire for carrying your bags and 1,000–2,000 for room service.

Opening and Closing Times

Rome's churches have unpredictable opening times; they are *not* open all the time. Most are open from about 7 to 12 and 3 to 7, but don't be surprised if the church you were especially keen on seeing is closed during these times. Many that are shut during the week can be visited on Sunday. Appropriate dress—no shorts—is required.

Banks are open weekdays from 8:30 to 1:30 and 3 or 3:30 to 4 or 4:30. Shops are open Monday through Saturday, 9:30 to 1 and 3:30 or 4 through 7 or 7:30. Many are closed Monday mornings from September through June and Saturday afternoons in July and August.

Getting Around

Although most of Rome's sights are in a relatively circumscribed area, the city is too large to be seen solely on foot. Take the Metro (subway), a bus, or a taxi to the area you plan to visit, and expect to do a lot of walking once you're there. Wear a pair of comfortable, sturdy shoes, preferably with rubber or crepe soles to cushion the impact of the *sampietrini* (cobblestones). Heed our advice on security and get away from the noise and polluted air of heavily trafficked streets by taking parallel streets whenever possible. You can buy transportation-route maps at newsstands and at ATAC (Rome's public transit authority) information and ticket booths. The free city map distributed by Rome EPT offices is good; it also shows Metro and bus routes, although bus routes are not always marked clearly.

By Metro This is the easiest and fastest way to get around, but it's limited in extent. The Metro opens at 5:30 AM, and the last trains leave the farthest station at 11:30 PM. There are two lines—A and B—which intersect at Termini Station. The fare is 1,000 lire. There are ticket booths at major stations, but elsewhere you must use ticket machines. It's best to buy single tickets or books of 10 at newsstands and tobacconists. The "BIG" daily tourist ticket, good on buses as well, costs 4,000 lire and is sold at Metro and ATAC ticket booths.

By Bus Orange ATAC city buses and tram lines run from about 6 AM to midnight, with skeleton (*notturno*) services on main lines through the night. Remember to board at the back and exit at the middle. The ticket, 1,200 lire, is valid on all ATAC bus lines for a total of 90 minutes. Buy it before boarding, and time-stamp it in the machine on the first bus you board. Tickets are sold at tobacconists and newsstands. A weekly tourist ticket costs 18,000 lire and is sold at ATAC booths. The BIG tourist ticket is also valid on the Metro for one day (*see above*).

By Taxi Taxis wait at stands and can also be called by phone, in which case you're charged a small supplement. The meter starts at 6,400 lire, a fixed rate for the first 3 kilometers (1.8 miles); there are supplements for service after 10 PM and on Sunday or holidays, as well as for each piece of baggage. Use only metered yellow or white cabs. To call a cab, telephone 3875, 3570, 4994, or 8433. **Radio Taxi** (tel. 06/3875) accepts American Express and Diners Club credit cards, but you must specify when calling that you will pay that way.

By Bicycle Pedaling through Villa Borghese, along the Tiber, and through the center of the city when traffic is light is a pleasant way to see the sights, but remember: Rome is hilly. (For rentals, *see* Sports in Chapter 3,Exploring Rome.)

By Scooter You can rent a moped or scooter and mandatory helmet at **Scoot-a-Long** (Via Cavour 302, tel. 06/678–0206) or **St. Peter's Moto** (Via di Porta Castello 43, tel. 06/687–5714).

Guided Tours

Orientation **American Express** (tel. 06/67641), **CIT** (tel. 06/47941), **Appian Line** (tel. 06/488–4151), and other operators offer three-hour tours in air-conditioned 60-passenger buses with English-speaking guides. There are four standard itineraries: "Ancient Rome" (including the Roman Forum and Colosseum), "Classic Rome" (including St. Peter's Basilica, Trevi Fountain, and the Janiculum Hill), "Christian Rome" (some major churches and the Catacombs), and "The Vatican Museums and Sistine Chapel." Most cost about 36,000 lire, but the Vatican Museums tour costs about 48,000 lire. American Express tours depart from Piazza di Spagna, and CIT from Piazza della Repubblica, both with some hotel pickups; Appian Line picks you up at your hotel.

American Express and other operators can provide a luxury car for up to three people, a limousine for up to seven, and a minibus for up to nine—all with English-speaking driver—but guide service is extra. A minibus costs about 450,000 lire for three hours. Almost all operators offer "Rome by Night" tours, with or without pizza or dinner and entertainment. You can book tours through travel agents.

The least-expensive organized sightseeing tour of Rome is run by **ATAC,** the municipal bus company. Tours leave from Piazza dei Cinquecento, in front of Termini Station, last about three hours, and cost about 10,000 lire. There's no running commentary, but you're given an illustrated guide with which you can easily identify the sights. Buy tickets at the ATAC information booth in front of Termini Station; there is at least one tour daily, departing at 2:30 (3:30 in summer). The least expensive sightseeing of all are the routes of Bus 119 downtown, Bus 56 across Rome to Trastevere, or the circle route of Tram 19. For each, the cost is 1,200 lire one way.

Special-Interest You can make your own arrangements (at no cost) to attend a public papal audience in the Vatican or at the pope's summer residence at Castel Gandolfo. Or you can book through **CIT** (tel. 06/47941), **Appian Line** (Via Barberini 109, tel. 06/488–4151), or **Carrani Tours** (Via Vittorio Emanuele Orlando 95, tel. 06/488–0510). These agencies take you by bus to the Vatican for the audience, showing you some sights along the way and returning you to or near your hotel, for about 36,000 lire. The excursion for the pope's noon blessing on summer Sundays at Castel Gandolfo costs about 40,000 lire.

Excursions Most operators offer half-day excursions to Tivoli to see the fountains and gardens of the Villa d'Este. **Appian Line's** (tel. 06/488–4151) and **CIT's** half-day tours to Tivoli include a visit to Hadrian's Villa, with its impressive Roman ruins. Most operators also have full-day excursions to Florence, Assisi, Pompeii, and Capri, among other places of interest.

Personal Guides You can arrange for a personal guide through **American Express** (tel. 06/67641); **CIT** (tel. 06/47941); or the main **EPT Tourist Information Office** (tel. 06/488–3748).

Walking If you have a reasonable knowledge of Italian, you can take advantage of the free guided visits and walking tours organized by Rome's cultural associations and the city council for museums and monuments. These usually take place on Sunday mornings. Programs are announced in the daily newspapers.

Credit Cards

The following credit card abbreviations are used: AE, American Express; DC, Diners Club; MC, MasterCard; V, Visa.

2 Portrait of Rome

The Colosseum

By H. V. Morton

This vivid description of the Colosseum appeared originally in H. V. Morton's 1957 classic, A Traveller in Rome.

The first sight of the Colosseum is highly gratifying. It reassures the most bewildered visitor. No one could mistake it for anything but a large shambles designed with the utmost skill to focus the attention of many thousands of people upon a small field of action, then to disperse them with the greatest possible efficiency.

The amazing thing about the Colosseum is the fact that it is built in a marsh, and that its stupendous weight has been resting for all these centuries upon artificial foundations set in water. This part of Rome is still waterlogged with springs which trickle down from the Esquiline Hill, as you can see today in the underground churches beneath S. Clemente. How the Colosseum was built on such a soil is a wonder of engineering, and I can well imagine that any architect might forsake all else in Rome to study the problems of this triumphant mass. In the year 1864 one of the periodic stories about buried treasure in the Colosseum was revived with success by a certain Signor Testa. He claimed to have a clue to "the Frangipani treasure" believed to have been concealed there in the Middle Ages when that family turned the amphitheatre into a fortress. Pope Pius IX became interested and gave permission for the excavations, which were followed with breathless interest by everyone in Rome. Nothing of intrinsic value was found, though the effort was not wasted as it gave Lanciani his only chance to examine the foundations of the Colosseum. He wrote that he saw "the upper belt of the substructures, arched like those of the ambulacra above ground; and underneath them a bed of concrete which must descend to a considerable depth." So beneath the visible

Itarches of the Colosseum are others, carrying the weight of the building on cores of the indestructible Roman concrete sunk into the water.

It was the Venerable Bede, writing in his monastery at Jarrow somewhere about AD 700, who first addressed the building as the Colosseum in the famous proverb that Byron translated as:

While stands the Colosseum, Rome shall stand;
When falls the Colosseum, Rome shall fall;
And when Rome falls—the world.

Bede had never been to Rome, but no doubt he had heard of the Colosseum from Saxon pilgrims and may even have preserved a saying current in Rome in those days.

I climbed all over the mighty monument, thinking that it is the most comprehensible ruin in Rome. It demands little imagination to rebuild it in its splendour and fill it with 80,000 spectators, with Caesar in the royal box, the senators in their privileged seats near the rails, the aristocracy, and the Vestal Virgins; then, ascending, to the mob in the highest seats of all, for the audience in the Colosseum was seated in strict rotation. There was an official called a *designator* who saw to it that people kept in their proper places. There were at various times dress regulations which had to be obeyed. Roman citizens were obliged to attend the games in the toga, and the magistrates and senators came in their official dress. This enormous gathering, rising in tiers and mostly clothed in white, must have presented a mighty spectacle, with the senators in their striped togas and red sandals, the consuls in their purple tunics, the ambassadors and members of the diplomatic corps in the dress of their various countries, the praetorian guard in full dress, and the emperor in his royal robes. High

above the gallery protruded stout masts
where sailors from the fleet at Misenum, who
had been trained in the manipulation of a vast
awning, swarmed among the ropes and pulleys as in some gigantic galley. Even with a
slight wind the sound of this *velarium* was
like thunder, and on gusty days it could not
be used at all. One can imagine what it must
have been like to walk through the deserted
Forum on a day of the games and to hear the
flapping of this great awning, then to be
pulled up by a savage roar of sound from
eighty thousand voices.

Such a gathering of people assembled to
enjoy suffering and death must have
been a fearful sight, and I remembered the
story of St. Augustine's friend, Alypius, who
was taken to the games against his will by a
number of fellow students. At first Alypius
shut his eyes and refused to look, but, hear-
ing a sudden savage shout, he opened his eyes
to see a gladiator beaten to his knees. His
heart filled with pity for the man, then as the
death blow was delivered he "drank down a
kind of savageness" and sat there, open-eyed
and initiated. With the exception of Seneca, not one of the writers of antiquity, not
even the kindly Horace and the gentle Pliny,
condemned the degradation of the amphitheater, and the world had to wait for Christianity before men had the courage and the
decency to close such places.

As I climbed about the broken tiers and
ledges, I thought of the organization which
fed this monstrous circle of savagery. All
over the empire officials trapped and brought
wild animals for the arena, and in the course
of centuries the number of noble beasts that
died to please the mob is said to have almost
exterminated certain species from the Roman world. It is said that the elephant disappeared from North Africa, the hippopotamus
from Nubia, and the lion from Mesopotamia.

Long before the Colosseum was built this slaughter of animals used to be the popular prelude to the combat of gladiators; one display occupied the morning and the other the afternoon. Sulla once exhibited 100 lions in the arena and this, Cicero says, was the first time these animals were allowed to roam about instead of being tethered to stakes. In 58 BC several crocodiles and the first hippopotamus to be seen in Rome were exhibited in a trench of water in the arena, and during a *venatio* attended by Cicero in 55 BC, 600 lions were slain and 18 elephants tried to break down the barriers in an attempt to escape. The only animal which roused any compassion in the heartless Roman mob was the elephant. Cicero says that this was due to a notion that it had something in common with Mankind; and the elder Pliny says that these animals, which had been procured by Pompey, "implored the compassion of the multitude by attitudes which surpass all description, and with a kind of lamentation bewailed their unhappy fate," until "the whole assembly rose in tears and showered curses on Pompey." Unfortunately, such pity did not go very deep, and for centuries to come the mob continued to watch the slaughter of elephants and every other kind of animal; indeed, as the empire declined these fearful shows became even more extravagant.

There were schools in Rome where men were trained to fight animals and to devise tricks to amuse and thrill the mob. Such men, known as *bestiarii* or *venatores*, were lower in rank than the gladiators. Criminals could be sentenced to join such establishments and to be trained in an arena with the animals. After the Colosseum was built, the animals destined for the amphitheater were kept in a zoo known as the Vivarium, on the neighboring Celian Hill. On the day of the

games they were taken under the amphitheater and placed in lifts, worked by pulleys
and windlasses, which pulled the cages up to
the arena.

The death of animals merely stimulated the
palate for the afternoon combat of men.
In imperial times there were four state
schools in which gladiators lived under strict
discipline. They were fed on a special diet and
trained in every kind of weapon from the
sword and the lance to the net and lassoo. The
professional gladiator, like the modern film
actor, was the idol of the crowd and, of
course, of some women. There is a wall-scrib-
ble in Pompeii which describes a certain gladiator as "the maiden's sigh." With good
fortune their popularity lasted longer than
that of a film star today, for we hear of old
warriors, the heroes of a hundred fights,
winning the "wooden sword," which was
handed to them in the arena as a badge of
honorable retirement. There was also a great
deal of money to be made.

In addition to the state schools, there were
numerous private *ludi*, where gladiators
were maintained at the expense of rich ama-
teurs or businessmen, who hired them out to
fulfil engagements all over the country, as
the promotors of bullfights today engage
matadores with their *cuadrilla*. The Colosseum could also be rented. A rich man, or a
politician anxious to curry favor, could organize games to take place in the Colosseum,
and while they were in progress he occupied a
place of honor, the *editoris tribunal*, a special
seat which has now disappeared.

The Vestal Virgins were the only women
allowed in the official seats, and if the empress attended the games, she sat with them.
Women were not encouraged, however, to attend the amphitheater, and could sit only in
the upper tiers with the *plebs*. In later times

they were allowed to fight and were sometimes pitted against each other as gladiators;
but this, like the woman matador of today,
was not usual.

How the Vestal Virgins, who were so care-
fully protected against the harder facts
of life, were expected to endure the games, I
do not know, and I have read that it was
sometimes necessary to move them to the
higher parts of the Colosseum where they
could not see so much. From the first moment
until the last, when a ghastly figure dressed
as Charon, or a denizen of the underworld,
appeared and tapped with a wooden mallet
the heads of those not yet dead, the "entertainment" can hardly have been fit for their
eyes, and that these cloistered women were
required to be officially present indicates one
of the great differences between the pagan
and the Christian world.

The gladiators paraded in carriages on a day
of the games, just as modern bullfighters do.
Arriving at the Colosseum, they lined up and
took part in the *paseo* to the sound of music,
and marched around the arena, with attendants following, bearing their weapons. When
they reached a point opposite the royal box,
they would fling up their right hands and give
their famous cry: "Hail Caesar, we about to
die salute you!"

The weapons were then inspected, and any
that had been tampered with were thrown
out. Sometimes the duellists were selected
by lot; sometimes experts in the use of different weapons would be matched against each
other, a swordsman against a man with a net
and a trident, and so forth. At a signal from
the emperor a series of life and death duels
began, while the band of trumpets, horns,
flutes, and a hydraulic organ, struck up and
added to the noise of excited thousands, and
the shouts of the instructors, who urged on

the fighters with bloodthirsty incitements and, if they were not really trying, used a whip on them.

The most merciful combats were those in which the beaten gladiator had the right to appeal for his life. If he had fought well, the crowd might save him from death, as they leaned forward with their thumbs up, a sign meaning *Mitte!* ("Let him go"), but if they wished to see him die, the thumbs would be turned down—*Jugula!* ("Kill him!"); and the master of the world, glancing around to interpret the wishes of the multitude, would give the signal of life or death.

No mercy, however, was possible in the combats known as the fight to the death, in which a company of gladiators fought until only one survived; and even more horrible than this were the noon interludes, before the serious contests began, when a crowd of miserable robbers, highwaymen, murderers, and others condemned to death, were driven into the arena and given weapons with which they were compelled to kill each other. The deaths of Christians in the arena in Nero's time, and later, were of this character, but as the Christians could not be expected to slay one another, wild beasts were let loose to do the killing. It is extraordinary to contrast the gravity and dignity of Roman life at its best with the hideous degradation of mind exhibited in the public amusements of Rome.

One of the most vivid impressions of the Colosseum is the account by Dion Cassius of an occasion when the crazy young Emperor Commodus, who wanted to be worshipped as the royal Hercules, appeared as a *bestiarius* in the arena. Dion Cassius was present in his official capacity as a senator, dressed in his robes and wearing a laurel wreath. He describes the young emperor, dressed as Mercury, shooting bears with his bow and arrow as he darted about the galleries of the amphitheater. Then, descending into the arena, Commodius slew a tiger, a sea lion, and an elephant. At intervals during these exploits the senators, ashamed to see the son of Marcus Aurelius lowering the imperial dignity, were nevertheless obliged to give certain ritual shouts or acclamations: "You are the master!"; "You are always victorious!" Then, says Dion Cassius, the emperor advanced towards the senatorial benches holding up the head of an animal he had just killed, and, with his dripping sword held aloft, "he shook his head without saying one word, as if by that action he intended to threaten us in the same manner as he had served the beast." Many of the senators were convulsed with laughter, but, as this might have cost them their lives, Dion Cassius says he quietly pulled some of the laurel leaves from his crown and chewed them and "advised those sitting near me to do the same."

R eading these ancient authors I had an idea that many of them disliked the games, but accepted them as a national institution and one that had the blessing of the head of the state. The Emperor Tiberius disliked them and made no secret of it, and so did Marcus Aurelius, who caused great offence by talking and dictating letters while he was seated in the royal box: but it was not until Christian times that opposition could make any real headway and the games gradually fell into disuse. The last games were probably a mere memory of the past, for Cassiodorus says that the wild beasts imported by Theodoric in 519 were a novelty to his contemporaries. The games held by Anicius Maximus in 523 are the last to be recorded. If the bones of horses and bulls discovered by professors in the Colosseum in 1878 belong to this occasion, it would appear that in later times it had become a bullring.

And so it became in the Middle Ages, with occasional plays and pageants. Then, with trees and weeds gaining upon it, robbers and hermits took up residence there, while witches and sorcerers made it the headquarters of the Black Art. It was here on a dark night that Benvenuto Cellini experienced his celebrated encounter with devils. With a Sicilian priest and a young boy from his studio, he went to the Colosseum to hold a seance. A magic circle was drawn, the proper incantations were made, and perfumes burnt; then, visible to the priest and the terrified boy, but not apparently to Cellini, the amphitheater became filled with demons. A million warlike men surrounded them, said the frightened lad, and his terror was shared by the priest, who trembled like a reed. Cellini says he also was afraid, but told them that all they saw was smoke and shadows. The boy shouted "The whole Colosseum is on fire, and the fire is upon us!", and refused to look again. Eventually they left as Matin bells were ringing, and on the way home the boy reported that a couple of the demons were still following them, sometimes frisking ahead or capering on the rooftops.

Centuries later the Georgians and Victorians claimed this same site to be the most romantic ruin in Rome. Upon the ancient stage stained with the blood of innumerable men and beasts our great-grandmothers put up their easels and sketched a shepherd and his goats near a broken marble pedestal. By that time trees and shrubs were growing where senators had once sat in official dignity, and hermits in the upper circles now added a touch of romance.

A botanist wrote a book on the flora of the Colosseum, noting 266 species, which investigators later increased to 420. It became the fashion to see the Colosseum by moonlight. Leaving the candlelight and the card tables,

the ices and the after-dinner sweetmeats,
satin and velvet would crowd into *carrozze*
and go by the light of a full moon to the fallen
giant.

"It is not possible to express the solemn grandeur of it," wrote Lady Knight in 1795. "The
moon entered the broken part and struck full
upon that which is most perfect, and as by
that light no small parts were seen, you could
almost believe that it was whole and filled
with spectators."

Here, later, Byron heard "the owl's long
cry." Dickens and Dr. Arnold, and a hundred
more, added their tributes to a scene of mel-
ancholy that had no equal in the world. Then,
as soon as Rome became the capital of Italy,
the Colosseum was weeded by archaeologists
and the 420 varieties were heartlessly torn
from their crevices. So it stands today, still
arousing wonder and incredulity: a colossus
in stone with a gash in its side from which
thousands of tons of travertine crashed in the
Middle Ages. If all the stones which once
filled that gigantic gap could fly back to their
original positions, the Palazzo Venezia, the
Palazzo Farnese and the Palazzo della
Cancelleria, and many more, would suddenly
disintegrate and vanish.

3 Exploring Rome

From ancient times, Romans have been piling the present on top of the past, blithely building, layering, and overlapping their more than 2,500 years of history to create the haphazard fabric of modern Rome. The result is a city where antiquity is taken for granted, where you can have coffee in a square designed by Bernini and go home to a Renaissance palace. Normal life in Rome is carried on in an extraordinary setting.

Don't be self-conscious in your wanderings about the city. Poke and pry under the surface of things. Walk boldly through gates that are just ajar to peek into the hidden world of Roman courtyards. But do it with a smile, to show the people you meet that you're truly interested in them. Warm and straightforward, the Romans are pleased to show you the nooks and crannies of their hometown.

The good-humored Romans have their problems, of course. The city is noisy, polluted, afflicted with hellish traffic, and exasperatingly inefficient. But at least the traffic problem is being tackled. Sizable areas of the city center have been designated for pedestrians only. The pollution problem is less easy to cure, and far too many of the monuments you will want to see are shielded in fine green netting, while work proceeds on cleaning and repairing them.

Keep your sightseeing flexible. You'll have to plan your day to take into account the wide diversity of opening times—which will mean mixing classical sites with Baroque, museums with parks, the center with the environs. However you do it, be sure to take plenty of time off for simply sitting and observing the passing pageant of the city's teeming streets.

Inevitably, the environs of Rome are overshadowed by the five-star attractions of the Eternal City. However, the surrounding region, known as Lazio (Latium), has plenty to offer in its own right—ancient art and archaeology, medieval hill towns and abbeys, Renaissance pleasure gardens, lake and mountain scenery, and an easygoing pace, not to mention great local wines and homemade pasta. Intersperse city sightseeing with jaunts into the countryside. A breath of country air and a change of scenery can enhance your enjoyment of Rome and give you a new perspective on its many delights.

Our exploration of Rome is divided into 10 tours. We begin where Rome itself began, amid the ancient ruins, and follow with a look at the Vatican and its museums—two separate tours. The next six tours explore various places of interest in central Rome, while Tour 10 takes you on a short trip outside the city walls. With the exception of Tours 2 and 3, which concentrate on the Vatican, Tour 8, which explores the Villa Borghese, Tour 9, which crosses the Tiber to the Trastevere district, and Tour 10, out the Appian Way to the Catacombs, these Rome tours begin in or around Piazza Venezia.

The MuseidonCard, valid for two, four, or seven days and costing from 13,000 lire to 48,000 lire, provides entrance to city museums and some monuments. It's sold at participating museums, APT offices, and some hotels and tobacconists, but think twice before buying it because not many of the major museums are city run.

At the end of the chapter are three excursions into the surrounding countryside. Although all the places we suggest visiting could be seen on a day's trip from Rome, some itineraries combine several destinations and could be broken by an overnight stop somewhere along the way, to maintain an easy pace. If you're driving, you'll find good roads, but you may run into pockets of local traffic in the suburbs. Try not to schedule your excursions for Sundays, when the Romans make their weekly exodus and create traffic jams on their return.

A word of caution: Gypsy children, present around sites popular with tourists throughout Europe, are rife in Rome and are adept pickpockets. One modus operandi is to approach a tourist and proffer a piece of cardboard with writing on it. While the unsuspecting victim attempts to read the message *on* it, the gypsy children's hands are busy *under* it, making like piranhas with the contents of a purse. If you see such a group (recognizable by their unkempt appearance, often with cigarettes hanging from prepubescent mouths), do not even allow them near you—they are quick and know more tricks than you do. Also be aware of Italian perpetrators who ride by on motorbikes, grab the shoulder strap of your bag, and step on the gas. Keep your bag well under your arm, especially if you're walking on the street edge of the sidewalk, or wear a money belt. Don't carry more money than you need, and don't carry your passport unless you need it to exchange money.

Numbers in the margin correspond to points of interest on the Exploring Rome map.

Ancient Rome

Rome was built on seven hills. Its legendary founders, the twins Romulus and Remus, were abandoned as infants but were suckled by a she-wolf on the banks of the Tiber and adopted by a shepherd. Encouraged by the gods to build a city, the twins chose a site in 735 BC, fortifying it with a wall that has been identified by archaeologists digging on the Palatine, the first hill of Rome to be inhabited. During the building of the city, the brothers quarreled, and in a fit of anger Romulus killed Remus. Excavations on the Palatine and in the Forum area have revealed hard evidence of at least some aspects of the city's legendary beginnings.

The ruins on the two most historic hills—the Capitoline and the Palatine—mark the center of ancient Rome, capital of the classical world and center of a vast empire. The former hill held the seat of government, the Capitol, whose name is commemorated in every capital city in the world, as well as in government buildings, such as the Capitol in Washington, DC.

If you stand on the Capitoline and gaze out over the ruins of the Forum to the Palatine, with the Colosseum looming in the background, you can picture how Rome looked when it was the center of the known world. Imagine the Forum filled with immense, brightly painted temples. Picture the faint glow from the temple of Vesta, where the vestal virgins tended their sacred fire, and the glistening marble palace complex on the Palatine, its roof studded with statues, where the emperors and their retinues lived in incredible luxury. Then think of how the area looked in the Dark Ages, when Rome had sunk into malaria-ridden squalor.

The **Capitoline hill** is a good place to begin when exploring the city. Rome's first and most sacred temples stood here. The city's archives were kept in the Tabularium (hall of records), the tall, gray stone structure that forms the foundations of today's city hall, the **Palazzo Senatorio.** By the Middle Ages, the Campidoglio, as the hill was then known, had fallen into ruin. In 1537, Pope Paul III called on Michelangelo to restore it to grandeur, and the artist designed the ramp, the buildings on three sides of the **Campidoglio** Square, the slightly convex pavement and its decoration, and the pedestal for the bronze equestrian statue of Marcus Aurelius. A work of the 2nd century AD, the statue stood here from the 16th century to just recently, when it was removed for restoration and reinstallation in a more friendly environment inside the Palazzo dei Conservatori (*see below*). Eventually, a copy of the statue will occupy the original pedestal outdoors.

The palaces flanking the Palazzo Senatorio contain two museums, the **Museo Capitolino** and the **Palazzo dei Conservatori,** whose collections were assembled in the 15th century by Pope Sixtus V, one of the earliest of the great papal patrons of the arts. Those with a taste for Roman and Greek sculpture will appreciate both museums; others may find the collections dull but the setting impressive. Many of the statues were restored by overconscientious 18th- and 19th-century collectors who added heads and limbs with considerable abandon. Originally, almost all these works were brilliantly colored and gilded. Many of the works here and in Rome's other museums are copies of Greek originals. For hundreds of years, craftsmen of ancient Rome prospered by producing copies of Greek statues on order; they used a process called "pointing," by which exact copies could be made.

Portraiture, however, was one area in which the Romans outstripped the Greeks. The hundreds of Roman portrait busts in the **Museo Capitolino** are the highlight of a visit here. In the courtyard, the reclining river god is one of the "talk-

ing statues" to which ancient Romans affixed
anonymous political protests and satirical
barbs. The most interesting pieces, on display
upstairs, include the poignant *Dying Gaul* and
the delicate *Marble Faun,* which inspired novel-
ist Nathaniel Hawthorne's tale of the same
name. Then you'll come upon the rows of portrait busts, a kind of ancient *Who's Who,* though
rather haphazardly labeled. Look for cruel Caracalla, vicious Nero, and haughty Marcus Aurelius.

❷ Across the square is the **Palazzo dei Conservatori,** which contains similar treasures. The huge
head and hand in the courtyard are fragments of
a colossal statue of the emperor Constantine;
these immense effigies were much in vogue in
the later days of the Roman empire. The resplendent Salone dei Orazi e Curiazi upstairs is
a ceremonial hall with a magnificent gilt ceiling,
carved wooden doors, and 16th-century frescoes. Farther on, you'll see the famous *Capitoline Wolf,* a 6th-century BC Etruscan bronze;
the twins were added during the Renaissance to
adapt the statue to the legend of Romulus and
Remus. *Museo Capitolino and Palazzo dei
Conservatori, Piazza del Campidoglio, tel. 06/
671–02071. Admission: 10,000 lire. Open May–
Sept., Tues. 9–1:30 and 5–8, Wed.–Fri. 9–1:30,
Sat. 9–1:30 and 8–11, Sun. 9–1; Oct.–Apr.,
Tues. and Sat. 9–1:30 and 5–8, Wed.–Fri.
9–1:30, Sun. 9–1.*

❸ The Capitoline's church of **Aracoeli** was one of
the first in the city built by the emerging Christians. It's known for Pinturicchio's 16th-century
frescoes in the first chapel on the right and for a
much-revered wooden figure of the Christ
Child, kept in a small chapel in the sacristy.

The Campidoglio gardens offer the best view of
the sprawling ruins of ancient Rome. **Caesar's
Forum** lies below the garden, to the left of Palazzo Senatorio. It is the oldest of the Imperial
Fora, those built by the emperors, as opposed to
those built during the earlier, Republican period (6th–1st centuries BC), as part of the original
Roman Forum.

Across Via dei Fori Imperiali, the broad avenue
created by Premier Benito Mussolini for his tri-

Exploring Rome

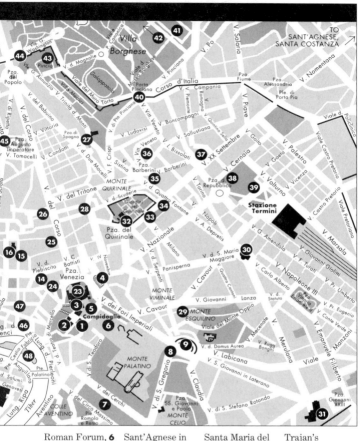

❹ umphal parades, are, from the left, **Trajan's Column,** in the base of which the emperor Trajan's ashes were buried, **Trajan's Forum,** with its huge semicircular market building, and the ruins of the **Forum of Augustus.**

Now turn your attention to the Roman Forum, in what was once a marshy valley between the Capitoline and Palatine hills. The shortest way down is Via San Pietro in Carcere—actually a flight of stairs descending to the church that ❺ stands over the **Mamertine Prison,** a series of gloomy, subterranean cells where Rome's vanquished enemies were finished off. Legend has it that St. Peter was held prisoner here and that he miraculously brought forth a spring of water in order to baptize his jailers. *Donation requested. Open daily 9–12:30, 2–7:30.*

From the main entrance on Via dei Fori Imperiali, descend into the extraordinary ar- ❻ chaeological complex that is the **Roman Forum.** This was the civic heart of Republican Rome, the austere Rome that preceded the hedonistic society that grew up under the emperors in the 1st to the 4th century AD. Today it seems no more than a baffling series of ruins, marble fragments, isolated columns, a few worn arches, and occasional paving stones. Yet it once was filled with stately and extravagant buildings— temples, palaces, shops—and people from all corners of the world. What you see are the ruins of almost 900 years, from about 500 BC to AD 400. As the original buildings became too small or old-fashioned, they were pulled down and replaced by more lavish structures. Making sense of these scarred stones is not easy; you may want just to wander along, letting your imagination dwell on Julius Caesar, Cicero, and Mark Antony, who delivered the funeral address in Caesar's honor from the rostrum just left of the Arch of Septimius Severus. *Entrances on Via dei Fori Imperiali, Piazza Santa Maria Nova, and Via di San Gregorio, tel. 06/699–0110. Admission: 10,000 lire. Open Apr.–Sept., Mon., Wed.–Sat. 9–6, Tues. and Sun. 9–1; Oct.– Mar., Mon., Wed.–Sat, 9–3, Tues. and Sun. 9–1.*

Leave the Forum by the exit at Arco di Tito
(Arch of Titus), which is at the end of the Forum
away from the Capitoline. From here, the Cli-
vus Palatinus, an ancient path, leads up the Palatine hill, where the emperors built their
palaces. From the belvedere you can see the **Circus Maximus,** where more than 300,000 spectators could watch chariot and horse races while
the emperors looked on from this very spot. The
Italian garden on the Palatine was laid out during the Renaissance. Leaving the Palatine by
way of the Via di San Gregorio exit, you'll come
upon the imposing **Arch of Constantine,** erected
in AD 315 to commemorate Constantine's victory
over Maxentius.

Just beyond is the **Colosseum,** the most famous
monument of ancient Rome. Begun by the
Flavian emperor Vespasian in AD 72, it was inau-
gurated by Titus eight years later with a 100-
day program of games and shows. On the opening day alone, 5,000 wild beasts perished in the
arena. More than 50,000 spectators could crowd
into the 573-yard circumference, which was
faced with marble and boasted an ingenious system of awnings to shade them from the sun.
Originally known as the Flavian Amphitheater,
in later centuries it came to be called the Colosseum, after a colossal gilded bronze statue of
Nero that stood nearby. It served as a fortress
during the 13th century and then as a quarry
from which materials were filched to build
sumptuous Renaissance churches and palaces.
Finally it was declared sacred by the popes, in
memory of the many Christians believed mar-
tyred there. You must pay admission to the upper levels. *Piazza del Colosseo, tel. 06/700–
4261. Admission free; admission to upper levels: 6,000 lire. Open Mon., Tues., Thurs.–Sat.
9–one hour before sunset, Wed. and Sun. 9–1.*

Behind the Colosseum at the Colle Oppio
(Oppian Hill) on the Esquiline Hill is what's left
of Nero's fabulous **Domus Aurea,** a sumptuous
palace later buried under Trajan's Baths.

Time Out   About half a block from the Colosseum is **Pas-
qualino,** a reasonably priced neighborhood
trattoria with a few sidewalk tables with a view

of the arena's marble arches. (Via Santi Quattro 66. Closed Mon.)

If you head back toward Piazza Venezia on Via dei Fori Imperiali, you can get a good look at the Imperial Fora and Trajan's Market.

The Vatican

While the ancient Roman emperors presided over the decline of their empire, a vibrant new force emerged. Christianity came to Rome, the seat of the popes was established over the tomb of St. Peter, and the Vatican became the spiritual focus of the Roman Catholic Church. There are two principal reasons for seeing the Vatican. One is to visit St. Peter's, the largest church in the world and the most overwhelming architectural achievement of the Renaissance. The other is to visit the Vatican Museums, which contain collections of staggering richness and diversity, including, of course, the Sistine Chapel. There's little point in trying to take it all in on just one visit. See St. Peter's first, and come back later to see the Vatican Museums.

⑩ Start at **Castel Sant'Angelo,** which guarded the Vatican for hundreds of years. One of Rome's most beautiful bridges, **Ponte Sant'Angelo,** spans the Tiber in front of the fortress and is studded with copies of the graceful angels designed by Giovanni Lorenzo Bernini (1598–1680). The distinctive silhouette of Castel Sant'Angelo is a throwback to its original function; it was built as a mausoleum, or tomb, for the Emperor Hadrian in AD 135. By the 6th century, it had been transformed into a fortress, and it remained the military stronghold of Rome and a refuge for the popes for almost 1,000 years.

According to legend, the castle got its name during the plague of 590, when Pope Gregory the Great, passing by in a religious procession, had a vision of an angel sheathing its sword atop the stone ramparts. He interpreted this as a sign that the plague would end immediately, and, after it did, he had a chapel built on the highest level of the fortress, where he had seen the angel. Visit the lower levels, the base of Hadrian's mausoleum, and then climb ancient ramps and narrow staircases to explore the castle's courtyards and frescoed halls; the collection of antique arms and armor; and the open loggia, where there's a café. Climb to the upper terraces for views of the city's rooftops and the lower bastions of the castle, as well as of the Passetto, the fortified corridor connecting Castel Sant'Angelo with the Vatican. *Lungotevere Castello 50, tel. 06/687–5036. Admission: 8,000 lire. Open Apr.–Sept., Mon.–Sat. 9–7, Oct.–Mar., Mon.–Sat. 9–6, Sun. 9–noon. Closed 2nd and 4th Mon. of month.*

From Castel Sant'Angelo, turn right onto Via della Conciliazione, a broad, rather soulless avenue conceived by Mussolini in the 1930s to celebrate the "conciliation" between the Vatican and the Italian government under the Lateran Pact of 1929. The pact ended 60 years of papal protest against the Italian state, which the Vatican had never recognized. Indeed, after Italian troops wrested control of Rome from the pope in 1870 to make it the capital of a newly united Italy, the popes refused to leave the Vatican.

The Via della Conciliazione approach to St. Peter's gives your eye time to adjust to the enormous dimensions of the square and the church, although the intent of Baroque artist Bernini, who designed the square, was to surprise the visitor emerging suddenly from shadowy alleys into the square's immense space and full light.

⓫ **Piazza San Pietro** (St. Peter's Square) is one of Bernini's masterpieces, completed after 11 years' work—a relatively short time in those days, considering the vastness of the job. The square can hold as many as 400,000 people and is surrounded by a pair of quadruple colonnades, which are topped by a balustrade and 140 statues of saints. Look for the two stone disks set into the pavement on each side of the obelisk, between the obelisk and the fountains. If you stand on one disk, the colonnades seem to consist of a single row of columns.

⓬ The history of **St. Peter's** goes back to the year AD 319, when the emperor Constantine built a basilica here over the site of the tomb of St. Peter. The original church stood for more than

1,000 years, undergoing a number of restorations, until it threatened to collapse. Reconstruction began in 1452 but was soon abandoned due to a lack of funds. In 1506 Pope Julius II instructed the architect Donato Bramante (1444–1514) to raze the existing structure and build a new and greater basilica, but it wasn't until 1626 that the new church was completed and dedicated. Five of Italy's greatest Renaissance artists died while working on it—Bramante, Raphael, Peruzzi, Antonio Sangallo the Younger, and Michelangelo. Bramante outlined a basic plan for the church and built the massive pillars that were to support the dome. After his death in 1514, his successors made little progress with the work and altered his master plan. In 1546 Pope Paul III more or less forced the aging Michelangelo to take on the job of completing the building. Michelangelo returned to Bramante's ground plan and designed the dome to cover the crossing, but his plans, too, were modified after his death. Still the result is breathtaking. As you approach the church, look at the people going in and out of the portico, and note the contrast between their size and the immense scale of the building. Now climb the broad steps and enter the portico. Notice Filarete's 15th-century bronze doors, salvaged from the old basilica.

Persons wearing shorts, miniskirts, sleeveless T-shirts, or other revealing clothing (it's advisable for women to carry a scarf to cover bare upper arms) will not be allowed into St. Peter's. If you pass inspection, pause a moment, once inside, to consider the size of this immense temple. Look at the massive pillars, the holy-water stoups borne by colossal cherubs, the distance to the main altar. Look for the brass inscriptions in the central marble pavement, indicating the approximate length of the world's principal Christian churches, all of which fall far short of St. Peter's. The chapel immediately to your right holds Michelangelo's *Pietà*, one of the world's most famous statues. It is now behind shatterproof glass, after a serious incident of vandalism (and a masterful restoration in the Vatican workshops). This is the only sculpture Michelangelo ever signed, although the signature—on the sash across the Virgin's chest—is too high up behind the glass to be seen.

Four massive piers support the dome at the crossing, where the mighty Bernini *baldacchino* (canopy), made of bronze stripped from the Pantheon by order of the Barberini Pope Urban VIII, rises high above the papal altar. The pope celebrates mass here, over the grottoes holding the tombs of many of his predecessors and over what is believed to be the tomb of St. Peter, deep in the excavations under the foundations of the original basilica. A very old bronze statue of the saint stands at the last pillar on the right before the crossing, its foot worn and burnished by the kisses of the faithful over the centuries. Beautiful bronze vigil lights flicker around the ceremonial entrance to the crypt in front of the papal altar. In the niche below is an antique casket containing the *pallia* (bands of white wool conferred by the pope on archbishops as a sign of authority). The splendid gilt-bronze throne above the altar in the apse was designed by Bernini and contains a wooden-and-ivory chair that St. Peter was supposed to have used, though in fact it dates back no further than the Middle Ages. A copy of the chair is in the Treasury.

Stop in to see the small collection of Vatican treasures in the little **museum** in the sacristy, among them priceless antique chalices and the massive 15th-century bronze tomb of Pope Sixtus V by Antonio Pollaiuolo (1429–98). *Admission: 3,000 lire. Open Apr.–Sept., daily 9–6:30; Oct.–Mar., daily 9–5:30.*

Save the visit to the **Vatican Grottoes,** to see the tombs of the popes, for last. The only exit from the grottoes leads outside St. Peter's, near the entrance to the roof and dome. *Entrance at St. Longinus Pier but alternatively at one of the other piers. Admission free. Open Apr.–Sept., daily 7–6; Oct.–Mar., daily 7–5.*

Take the elevator or climb the stairs to the **roof** of the church, an interesting landscape of domes and towers. From here, climb a short interior staircase to the base of the dome for a dove's-eye view of the interior of the church. And from here, it's a taxing climb to the lantern—the architectural term for the delicate structure crowning the dome; the stairs are steep and narrow and one-way only, so there's no turning back. We emphasize that it's a strenuous, claustrophobic climb. Those who make it are rewarded with views embracing the Vatican gardens and all Rome. *Entrance to roof and dome in courtyard on left as you leave the church. Admission: 6,000 lire if you use elevator to roof, 5,000 if you use stairs. Open Apr.– Sept., daily 8–6; Oct.–Mar., daily 8–5.*

For many, a **papal audience** is a highlight of a trip to Rome. The pope holds mass audiences on Wednesday mornings at 11, in a modern audience hall. Rarely, on special occasions during the summer, a second audience may be held in St. Peter's Square. You must apply for tickets in advance, and it may be easier to arrange for them through a travel agency. Of course, you can avoid the formalities by seeing the pope when he makes his weekly appearance at the window of the Vatican Palace, every Sunday at noon when he is in Rome, to address the crowd and give a blessing. On summer Sundays he may give the blessing at his summer residence at Castel Gandolfo. *For audience tickets, apply in writing well in advance to the Prefettura della Casa Pontificia, 00120 Vatican City, indicating the date you prefer, the language you speak, and the hotel where you will be staying; or go to the prefecture yourself through the bronze door in the right-hand colonnade, tel. 06/6982. Open Mon. and Tues. 9–1 for the Wed. audience, though last-minute tickets may not be available. You can also pick up free tickets at the North American College, Via dell'Umiltà 30, tel. 06/678–9184, or through Santa Susanna American Church, Piazza San Bernardo, tel. 06/482–7510. For a fee, travel agencies make arrangements that include transportation.*

The Vatican Museums

The Vatican Palace, the residence of the popes on and off since 1377, is made up of several interlocking buildings containing 1,400 rooms, chapels, and galleries. The pope and his household occupy only a small part of the palace, most of which is given over to the Vatican Library and Museums. The main entrance to the museums,

on Viale Vaticano, is a long walk from Piazza San
Pietro, but there is bus service between the
square and a secondary museum entrance. It
goes through the Vatican gardens and costs
2,000 lire, and although it deposits you at a side
entrance, it saves a lot of walking and allows a
glimpse of some of Vatican City that would be
off-limits otherwise. A two-hour jaunt through
the pope's backyard, half by bus and half on foot,
is possible by taking the Vatican gardens tour.
*Bus service 8:45–12:45 on the half-hour, except
Sun. and Wed. Tour of Vatican gardens Mon.,
Tues., and Thurs.–Sat. Cost: 16,000 lire. Tickets are available at the Vatican Information Office in Piazza San Pietro. It's best to reserve two
or three days in advance.*

Time Out Borgo Pio, a street near St. Peter's Square, has
several trattorias offering economical tourist
menus. For about 20,000 lire you can have a sim-
ple meal at **Il Pozzetto** (Borgo Pio 167. Closed
Mon.).

⓭ The collections of the **Vatican Museums** are immense, covering about 4½ miles of displays.
Special posters at the entrance and throughout
the museum plot a choice of four color-coded
itineraries, the shortest taking approximately
90 minutes and the longest five hours. You can
rent taped English commentary explaining the
Sistine Chapel and the Raphael Rooms. You're
free to photograph what you like, although if
you want to use a flash, tripod, or other special
equipment, you have to get permission. The
main entrance is on Viale Vaticano and can be
reached by the No. 49 bus from Piazza Cavour,
which stops right in front; on foot from the No.
81 bus or No. 19 tram, which stop at Piazza Risorgimento; or from the Ottaviano stop on the
Metro Line A. Pick up a leaflet at the main entrance to the museums in order to see the overall
layout. The Sistine Chapel, the main attraction
for most visitors, is at the far end of the complex, and the leaflet charts two abbreviated itineraries through other collections to reach it.
Don't miss the collections en route to the Sistine
Chapel; below we give some of the highlights.
*Viale Vaticano, tel. 06/698–3333. Admission:
13,000 lire; free on last Sun. of month. Open*

Easter week and July–Sept., weekdays 8:45–5 (no admission after 4), Sat. 8:45–2; Oct.–June (except Easter), Mon.–Sat. 9–2 (no admission after 1). Closed Sun. year-round, except last Sun. of month (open 9–2, admission free), and religious holidays: Jan. 1, Jan. 6, Feb. 11, Mar. 19, Easter Sun. and Mon., May 1, Ascension Thurs., Corpus Christi, June 29, Aug. 15–16, Nov. 1, Dec. 8, Dec. 25–26.

Among Vatican City's many riches, probably the single most important is the Sistine Chapel. However, unless you're following one of the two abbreviated itineraries, you'll begin your visit at the recently rearranged **Egyptian Museum** and go on to the **Chiaramonti** and **Pio Clementino Museums,** which are given over to classical sculptures (among them some of the best-known statues in the world—the *Laocoön,* the *Belvedere Torso,* and the *Apollo Belvedere*—works that, with their vibrant humanism, had a tremendous impact on Renaissance art). Next come the **Etruscan Museum** and three other sections of limited interest. All itineraries merge in the **Candelabra Gallery** and proceed through the **Tapestry Gallery,** which is hung with magnificent tapestries executed from Raphael's designs.

The **Gallery of Maps** is intriguing; the **Apartment of Pius V,** a little less so. After them you'll enter the **Raphael Rooms,** second only to the Sistine Chapel in artistic interest. In 1508, Pope Julius II employed Raphael Sanzio, on the recommendation of Bramante, to decorate the rooms with biblical scenes. Of the four rooms, the second and third were decorated mainly by Raphael; the others, by Giulio Romano and other assistants of Raphael. The lovely Loggia (covered balcony) was designed and frescoed by the master himself. Next you pass through the Chiaroscuro Room to the tiny **Chapel of Nicholas V,** aglow with frescoes by Fra Angelico (1387–1455), the Florentine monk whose sensitive paintings were guiding lights for the Renaissance. If your itinerary takes you to the **Borgia Apartments,** you'll see their elaborately painted ceilings, designed and partially executed by Pinturicchio (1454–1513). The Borgia Apartments have been given over to the Vatican's large, but not particularly interesting, collection of modern religious art, which continues at a lower level. Once you've seen the Borgia Rooms, you can skip the rest in good conscience and get on to the Sistine Chapel.

In 1508, while Raphael was put to work on his series of rooms, Pope Julius II commissioned Michelangelo to fresco the more than 10,000 square feet of the **Sistine Chapel** ceiling single-handedly. The task took four years of mental and physical anguish. It's said that for years afterward Michelangelo couldn't read anything without holding it up over his head. The result, however, was the masterpiece that you can now see, its colors cool and brilliant after recent restoration. Bring a pair of binoculars to get a better look at this incredible work, and if you want to study it, try to beat the tour groups by getting there early in the day. Some 20 years after completing the ceiling, Michelangelo was commissioned to paint the *Last Judgment* on the wall over the altar. The aged and embittered artist painted his own face on the wrinkled human skin in the hand of St. Bartholomew, below and to the right of the figure of Christ, which he clearly modeled on the *Apollo Belvedere*. Like the ceiling, the **Last Judgment** has been cleaned, surprising viewers with its clarity and color after restorers unveiled their work in April 1994.

After this experience, which can be marred by the crowds of tourists, you pass through some of the exhibition halls of the **Vatican Library.** Look in on Room X, Room of the Aldobrandini Marriage, to see its beautiful Roman frescoes of a nuptial rite. You can see more classical statues in the new wing and then, perhaps after taking a break at the cafeteria, go on to the **Pinacoteca** (Picture Gallery). It displays mainly religious paintings by such artists as Giotto, Fra Angelico, and Filippo Lippi. The **Raphael Room** holds his exceptional *Transfiguration, Coronation,* and *Foligno Madonna.*

In the **Pagan Antiquities Museum,** modern display techniques enhance another collection of Greek and Roman sculptures. The **Christian Antiquities Museum** has Early Christian and medieval art, while the **Ethnological Museum** shows art and artifacts from exotic places throughout the world. The complete itinerary ends with the **Historical Museum**'s collection of carriages, uniforms, and arms, which may still be temporarily closed in 1995.

In all, the Vatican Museums offer a staggering excursion into the realms of art and history. It's foolhardy to try to see all the collections in one day, and it's doubtful that anyone could be interested in everything on display. Simply aim for an overall impression of the collections' artistic and cultural riches.

Time Out Neighborhood trattorias that are far better and far less touristy than those opposite the Vatican Museum entrance include **Hostaria Dino e Toni** (Via Leone IV 60. Closed Sun.), where you can dine on typical Roman fare at reasonable prices, and **La Caravella,** which serves Roman specialties and has pizza on the lunch menu (Via degli Scipioni 32, corner Via Vespasiano, off Via Leone IV. Closed Thurs.).

Old Rome

A district of narrow streets with curious names, airy Baroque piazzas, and picturesque courtyards, Old Rome *(Vecchia Roma)* occupies the horn of land that pushes the Tiber westward toward the Vatican. It has been an integral part of the city since ancient times, and its position between the Vatican and the Lateran palaces, both seats of papal rule, put it in the mainstream of Rome's development from the Middle Ages onward. Today it's full of old artisans' workshops, trendy cafés and eating places, and offbeat boutiques. On weekends and summer evenings Old Rome is a magnet for crowds of young people.

14 Start at Piazza Venezia and take Via del Plebiscito to the huge Baroque **Il Gesù,** comparable only to St. Peter's for sheer grandeur. Inside it's encrusted with gold and precious marbles and topped by a fantastically painted ceiling that flows down over the pillars to become three-dimensional, merging with painted stucco figures in a swirling composition glorifying the Jesuit order. Then head for nearby Piaz-

⑮ za della Minerva to see **Santa Maria Sopra Minerva,** a Gothic church with some beautiful frescoes, in a side chapel, by Filippo Lippi (1406–69), the monk who taught Botticelli. The tomb of another great artist-monk, Fra Angelico (c.1400–1455), stands to the left of the altar. Bernini's charming elephant bearing an obelisk stands in the center of the piazza.

⑯ The huge brick building opposite is the **Pantheon,** one of the most harmonious and best-preserved monuments of antiquity. It was first erected in 27 BC by Augustus's general Agrippa and completely redesigned and rebuilt by Hadrian, who deserves the credit for this fantastic feat of construction. At its apex, the dome is exactly as tall as the walls, so that you could imagine it as the upper half of a sphere resting on the floor; this balance gives the building a serene majesty. The bronze doors are the original ones; most of the other decorations of gilt bronze and marble that covered the dome and walls were plundered by later Roman emperors and by the popes. The Pantheon gets light and air from the apex of the dome—another impressive feature of this remarkable edifice. *Piazza della Rotonda, tel. 06/654-3311. Admission free. Open Mon.–Sat. 9–2, Sun. 9–1.*

Time Out The area is ice-cream heaven, with some of Rome's best *gelaterie* (ice-cream parlors) within a few steps of one another. Romans consider nearby **Giolitti** superlative and take the counter by storm. Remember to pay the cashier first and hand the stub to the man at the counter when you order your cone. Giolitti has a good snack counter, too (*Via Uffizi del Vicario 40. Closed Mon.*).

From Piazza della Rotonda in front of the Pantheon, take Via Giustiniani onto Via della **⑰** Dogana Vecchia to the church of **San Luigi dei Francesi.** In the last chapel on the left are three stunning works by Caravaggio (1571–1610), the master of the heightened approach to light and dark. A light machine (operated with a couple of 100-lire coins) provides illumination to view the paintings. *Open Fri.–Wed. 7:30–12:30 and 3:30–7, Thurs. 7:30–12:30.*

In the church of **Sant'Agostino,** close by (Piazza
di Sant'Agostino), there is another Caravaggio
over the first altar on the left. Just beyond these
(18) churches is **Piazza Navona,** a beautiful Baroque
piazza that traces the oval of Emperor Domi-
tian's stadium. It still has the carefree air of the
days when it was the scene of Roman circus
games, medieval jousts, and 17th-century carni-
vals. Bernini's splashing **Fountain of the Four
Rivers,** with an enormous rock squared off by
statues representing the four corners of the
world, makes a fitting centerpiece. Behind it
(19) stands the church of **Sant'Agnese in Agone.** Its
Baroque facade is by Francesco Borromini
(1599–1667), a contemporary and sometime rival of Bernini. One story has it that the Bernini
statue nearest the church is hiding its head because it can't bear to look upon the inferior Borromini facade; in fact, the facade was built after
the fountain, and the statue hides its head because it represents the Nile River, whose source
was unknown until relatively recently.

Time Out   The sidewalk tables of the **Tre Scalini** café offer a
grandstand view of the piazza. This place in-
vented the *tartufo,* a luscious chocolate ice-
cream specialty (Piazza Navona 30. Closed
Wed.).

Leaving Piazza Navona by way of the Corsia
Agonalis, the street opposite Tre Scalini, you'll
see the 17th-century **Palazzo Madama,** now the
Senate, on Corso Rinascimento. To the right, at
the end of the street, the huge church of
(20) **Sant'Andrea della Valle** looms mightily over a
busy intersection. Puccini set the first act of his
opera *Tosca* here.

Now make your way through side streets to
(21) **Campo dei Fiori.** Once the scene of public execu-
tions (including that of philosopher-monk
Giordano Bruno, whose statue broods in the
center), it now holds one of Rome's busiest, most
colorful morning food markets. *Mon.–Sat. 8–2.*

Continue on to Piazza Farnese, where Michelan-
(22) gelo had a hand in building **Palazzo Farnese,** now
the French Embassy and perhaps the most
beautiful of the Renaissance palaces in Rome.
(Puccini set the second act of *Tosca* here.) The

twin fountains in the piazza are made with basins of Egyptian granite from the Baths of Caracalla. Behind Palazzo Farnese, turn onto Via Giulia, where you'll see some elegant palaces (step inside the portals to take a look at the courtyards), old churches, and a number of antiques shops.

The Spanish Steps and the Trevi Fountain

The walk up Via del Corso from Piazza Venezia takes you to Rome's classiest shopping streets and to two visual extravaganzas: the Spanish Steps and the Trevi Fountain.

㉓ Start at the **Vittorio Emanuele Monument** in Piazza Venezia. Rome's most flamboyant landmark, it was erected in the late 19th century to honor Italy's first king, Vittorio Emanuele II, and the unification of Italy. This vast marble monument, said to resemble a wedding cake or a Victorian typewriter, houses the **Tomb of the Unknown Soldier,** with its eternal flame. Although the monument has been closed to the public for many years, plans are in the works to reopen it; the views from the top of the steps are among Rome's best.

㉔ On the left, as you look up the Corso, is **Palazzo Venezia,** a blend of medieval solidity and Renaissance grace. It contains a good collection of paintings, sculptures, and objets d'art in handsome salons, some of which Mussolini used as his offices. Notice the balcony over the main portal, from which Il Duce addressed huge crowds in the square below. *Via del Plebiscito 118, tel. 06/ 679–8865. Admission: 8,000 lire. Open Tues.– Sat. 9–1:30, Sun. 9–12:30.*

Along the Corso are some fine old palaces and a church or two. Detour to the left to the church of
㉕ **Sant'Ignazio,** where what seems to be the dome is really an illusionist canvas. Put some coins in the light machine to illuminate the dazzling frescoes on the vault of the nave. Next you'll come to
㉖ Piazza Colonna, named for the ancient **Column of Marcus Aurelius,** with its extraordinarily detailed reliefs spiraling up to the top.

Time Out   **Alfio,** on the corner of Via Bergamaschi, is popular for a stand-up lunch of sandwiches at the counter or a more relaxing meal in the upstairs dining room (Via della Colonna Antonina 33. Closed Sun.).

From Largo Goldoni, on Via del Corso, you get a head-on view of the Spanish Steps and the church of Trinità dei Monti as you start up Via Condotti, an elegant and expensive shopping street. Look for the historic **Caffè Greco** on the left. More than 200 years old, it was the haunt of Goethe, Byron, and Liszt; now it's a hangout for well-dressed ladies carrying Gucci bags.

27   Piazza di Spagna and the **Spanish Steps** get their names from the Spanish Embassy to the Holy See (the Vatican), opposite the American Express office, though they were built with French funds. This was once the core of Rome's bohemian quarter, especially favored by American and British artists and writers in the 18th and 19th centuries. At the center of the square is Bernini's **Fountain of the Barcaccia** (Old Boat), and just to the right of the steps is the house where Keats and Shelley lived. Sloping upward in broad curves, the Spanish Steps are perfect for socializing, and they draw huge crowds on weekend and holiday afternoons. From mid-April to early May, the steps are blanketed with azaleas in bloom.

From the narrow end of the piazza, take Via Propaganda Fide to Sant'Andrea delle Fratte, swerving left on Via del Nazareno, then crossing busy Via del Tritone to Via della Stamperia.
28   This street leads to the **Trevi Fountain,** one of Rome's most spectacular fountains when it's gushing. It was featured in the 1954 film *Three Coins in the Fountain*. And legend has it that you can ensure your return to Rome by tossing a coin in the fountain. Unfortunately, legend doesn't tell you how to cope with the souvenir vendors and aggressive beggars who are looking for a share of your change.

Historic Churches

Three churches are the highlights of this walk, two of them major basilicas with roots in the ear-

ly centuries of Christianity. Not far from Piazza
Venezia and the Roman Forum off Via Cavour is
㉙ the church of **San Pietro in Vincoli.** Look for Via
San Francesco da Paola, a street staircase that
passes under the old Borgia palace and leads to
the square in front of the church. Inside are St.
Peter's chains (under the altar) and Michelangelo's *Moses*, a powerful statue almost as
famed as his frescoes in the Sistine Chapel. The
Moses was destined for the tomb of Julius II, but
Michelangelo was driven to distraction by the
interference of Pope Julius and his successors,
and the tomb was never finished. The statue, intended as part of the tomb, is a remarkable
sculpture and a big tourist attraction, but crass
commercialism has ruined the starkly majestic
effect of this memorial. The church is usually
jammed with tour groups, and the monument itself is a front for a large and ugly souvenir shop.

㉚ Continue along Via Cavour to **Santa Maria
Maggiore,** one of Rome's oldest and most beautiful churches. Built on the spot where a 3rd-cen-
tury pope witnessed a miraculous midsummer
snowfall, it is resplendent with gleaming mosaics—those on the arch in front of the main altar
date from the 5th century; the apse mosaic dates
from the 13th century—and an opulent carved
wood ceiling supposed to have been gilded with
the first gold brought from the New World.

Via Merulana runs straight from Santa Maria
Maggiore to the immense cathedral of Rome,
㉛ **San Giovanni in Laterano,** where the early
popes once lived and where the present pope
still officiates in his capacity as Rome's bishop.
The towering facade and Borromini's cool Baroque interior emphasize the majesty of its pro-
portions.

The adjoining **Lateran Palace,** once the popes'
official residence and still technically part of the
Vatican, now houses the offices of the Rome Dio-
cese and the **Vatican Historical Museum** (admission 6,000 lire; open first Sun. of each month,
8:45–1). Restoration of the frescoes in the Bene-
diction Loggia, damaged by a 1993 terrorist
bomb, continues. Across the street, opposite
the Lateran Palace, a small building houses the
Scala Santa (Holy Stairs), claimed to be the

staircase from Pilate's palace in Jerusalem. Circle the palace to see the 6th-century octagonal **Baptistery of San Giovanni,** forerunner of many similar buildings throughout Italy, and Rome's oldest and tallest obelisk, brought from Thebes and dating from the 15th century BC.

One more church awaits you just down Via Carlo Felice. **Santa Croce in Gerusalemme,** with a pretty Rococo facade and Baroque interior, shelters what are believed to be relics of the True Cross found by St. Helena, mother of the emperor Constantine and a tireless collector of holy objects.

The Quirinale and Piazza della Repubblica

Although this tour takes you from ancient Roman sculptures to early Christian churches, it's mainly an excursion into the 16th and 17th centuries, when Baroque art—and Bernini—triumphed in Rome. The **Quirinale** is the highest of Rome's seven original hills (the others are the Capitoline, Palatine, Esquiline, Viminal, Celian, and Aventine) and the one where ancient Romans and later the popes built their residences in order to escape the deadly miasmas and the malaria of the low-lying area around the Forum. **Palazzo del Quirinale,** the largest on the square, belonged first to the popes, then to Italy's kings, and is now the official residence of the nation's president. The fountain in the square boasts ancient statues of Castor and Pollux reining in their unruly steeds and a basin salvaged from the Roman Forum.

Along Via del Quirinale (which becomes Via XX Settembre) are two interesting little churches, each an architectural gem. The first you'll come upon is **Sant'Andrea,** a small but imposing Baroque church designed and decorated by Bernini, who considered it one of his finest works and liked to come here occasionally just to sit and enjoy it. The second is the church of **San Carlo alle Quattro Fontane** (Four Fountains) at the intersection. It was designed by Bernini's rival, Borromini, who created a building that is an intricate exercise in geometric perfection, all curves and movement.

35 Turn left down Via delle Quattro Fontane to a splendid 17th-century palace, **Palazzo Barberini.** Inside, the **Galleria Nazionale** offers fine works by Raphael (the *Fornarina*) and Caravaggio and a salon with gorgeous ceiling frescoes by Pietro da Cortona. Upstairs, don't miss the charming suite of rooms decorated in 18th-century fashion. *Via delle Quattro Fontane 13, tel. 06/481–4591. Admission: 6,000 lire. Open Tues.–Sat. 9–2, Sun. 9–1.*

Down the hill, Piazza Barberini has Bernini's graceful **Tritone Fountain,** designed in 1637 for the sculptor's munificent patron, Pope Urban VIII, whose Barberini coat of arms, featuring bees, is at the base of the large shell.

Time Out   Located on Via Barberini, next to a movie house, **Italy Italy** offers the Italian version of fast food, tasty and inexpensive (Via Barberini 19. Closed Sun.).

---

36 Via Veneto winds its way upward from Piazza Barberini past **Santa Maria della Concezione,** a Capuchin church famous for its crypt, where the skeletons and assorted bones of 4,000 dead monks are artistically arranged in four macabre chapels. *Via Veneto 27, tel. 06/462850. Donation requested. Open daily 9–noon, 3–6.*

The avenue curves past the American Embassy and Consulate; the luxurious Excelsior Hotel; and Doney's and the Café de Paris, famous from the days of la dolce vita in the 1950s. At the U.S. Embassy, take Via Bissolati to Piazza San **37** Bernardo. The church of **Santa Maria della Vittoria,** on the corner, is known for Bernini's sumptuous Baroque decoration of the Cornaro Chapel, an exceptional fusion of architecture, painting, and sculpture, in which the *Ecstasy of St. Theresa* is the focal point. The statue represents a mystical experience in what some regard as very earthly terms. This could be a good point at which to rest.

An interesting side trip from Piazza San Bernardo takes you to the Early Christian churches of **Sant'Agnese** and **Santa Costanza,** about a mile beyond the old city walls. Take bus No. 36, 37, 60, or 136 along Via Nomentana to get there. Santa Costanza, a church-in-the-round, has vaults decorated with bright 4th-century mosaics. The custodian of the catacomb of Sant'Agnese accompanies you up the hill to see it. Art buffs should make this side trip; others may find it unrewarding. *Via di Sant'Agnese, tel. 06/832–0743. Admission to Sant'Agnese catacombs: 6,000 lire. Admission to Santa Costanza is free, but a tip is in order if you do not buy a ticket to Sant'Agnese. Open Mon., Wed., Thurs.–Sat. 9–noon and 4–6, Tues. 9–noon, Sun. 4–6.*

From Piazza San Bernardo, it's not far to Piazza della Repubblica, where the pretty **Fountain of the Naiads,** a turn-of-the-century addition, features voluptuous bronze ladies wrestling happily with marine monsters. On one side of the square is an ancient Roman brick facade, which marks the church of **Santa Maria degli Angeli,** adapted by Michelangelo from the vast central chamber of the colossal Baths of Diocletian, built in the 4th century AD. The baths were on such a grandiose scale that the church and its former monastery, around the corner to the right, account for only part of the area they occupied. Inside the church, take a good look at the eight enormous columns of red granite; these are the original columns of the baths' central chamber and are 45 feet high and more than 5 feet in diameter.

The collections of ancient Roman art of the **Museo Nazionale Romano** are now divided among the old museum in the former monastery of Santa Maria degli Angeli (entrance behind the church); a new museum in the Palazzo Massimo (the peach-colored building across the square from the old museum); and the small Planetario annex (next to the church in a building that was part of the ancient baths but served more recently as a movie theater). Another annex, Piazza Navona, will open this year. In addition to the statues in the Planetario, most of the museum's sculpture, including the *Ludovisi Throne,* the *Lancellotti Discus Thrower,* and the *Castelporziano Discus Thrower,* is destined for Palazzo Massimo. A delightful fresco from Empress Livia's villa outside Rome, depicting a garden in bloom, is being restored and is not on view. *Museo Nazionale Romano: Monastery of Santa Maria degli Angeli, Viale E. De Nicola 79, tel. 06/488–0530. Admission: 3,000 lire. Open Tues.–Sat. 9–2, Sun. 9–1. Palazzo Massimo, Piazza dei Cinquecento, admission and hours not available at press time; Planetario, admission free, open daily 10–1, 3–5.*

The Villa Borghese to the Ara Pacis

A half-mile walk northwest from Piazza della Repubblica up Via Orlando and Via Vittorio Veneto leads to **Porta Pinciana** (Pincian Gate), one of the historic city gates in the Aurelian Walls surrounding Rome. The Porta itself was built in the 6th century AD, about three centuries after the walls were built to keep out the barbarians. These days it is one of the entrances to the **Villa Borghese,** Rome's large 17th-century park, built as the pleasure gardens of the powerful Borghese family.

Once inside the park, turn right up Viale del Museo Borghese and make for the **Galleria Borghese,** which holds the family art collection. At press time, the gallery was undergoing extensive renovations, so parts of it may be closed. There is a sculpture collection on the first floor, where you can see Canova's famous statue of Pauline Borghese, wife of Camillo Borghese and sister of Napoleon. Officially known as *Venus Vincitrix*, it is really a depiction of a haughty (and very seductive) Pauline, lying provocatively on a Roman sofa. The next two rooms hold two important Baroque sculptures by Bernini: *David* and *Apollo and Daphne.* In each you can see the vibrant attention to movement that marked the first departure from the Renaissance preoccupation with the idealized human form. Daphne is being transformed into a laurel tree while fleeing from a lecherous Apollo: Twigs sprout from her fingertips while her pursuer recoils in amazement. The gallery's important picture collection has been moved to the large San Michele a Ripa complex in Trastevere, where the paintings are now hung in a former church; it will probably be there through 1995. *San Michele a Ripa complex: Via di San Michele 22, tel. 06/581–6732. Admission: 4,000*

*lire. Open Tues.–Sat. 9–7, Sun. 9–1. During
renovation, use the Galleria Borghese entrance
off Via Raimondi. Tel. 06/858577. Admission:
4,000 lire. Open May–Sept., Tues.–Sat. 9–7,
Sun. 9–1; Oct.–Apr., Tues.–Sat. 9–2, Sun. 9–1.*

From the Galleria Borghese, if you cross the
park taking Viale dell'Uccelleria and then go
left on Viale del Giardino Zoologico, you will
42 come to the **Galleria Nazionale d'Arte Moderna**
(National Gallery of Modern Art), a large white
building boasting Italy's leading collection of
20th-century works. *Viale delle Belle Arti 131,
tel. 06/322–4151. Admission: 8,000 lire. Open
Tues.–Sat. 9–2, Sun. 9–1. (During frequent
temporary exhibitions, open Tues.–Sat. 9–7,
Sun. 9–1.)*

Close by is the **Museo di Villa Giulia,** housing
one of the world's great Etruscan collections.
The villa is a former papal summer palace set in
lovely gardens. This is the place to study the
strange, half-understood Etruscan civilization,
for here are magnificent terra-cotta statues,
figurines, jewelry, household implements, sarcophagi—a whole way of life on display. Among
the most precious gems are the *Apollo of Veio*
and the *Sarcophagus of the Sposi.* When you
have had your fill of these treasures, step out
into the nymphaeum (the architectural term for
this place of cool recesses and fern-softened
fountains) and take a close look at the full-scale
reconstruction of an Etruscan temple in the garden. *Piazza di Villa Giulia 9, tel. 06/320–1951.
Admission: 8,000 lire. Open Wed. 9–7, Tues.
and Thurs.–Sat. 9–2, Sun. 9–1.*

43 The **Pincio** is an extension of Villa Borghese,
with gardens on a terrace overlooking much of
Rome. It was laid out by the early 19th-century
architect Valadier as part of his overall plan for
Piazza del Popolo. The Pincio offers a superb
view, absolutely spectacular when there is a fine
sunset, and it's also a vantage point from which
you can study Valadier's arrangement of **Piazza
del Popolo.**

This is one of Rome's largest squares and a traditional place for mass meetings and rallies. At
the center, four dignified stone lions guard an
obelisk relating the life and times of Ramses II

in the 13th century BC. Next to the 400-year-old
(44) Porta del Popolo, Rome's northern city gate,
stop in at the church of **Santa Maria del Popolo** to
see a pair of Caravaggios and some Bernini
sculptures in a rich Baroque setting.

From here, it's a short walk down Via Ripetta to
the large **Augusteum,** the mausoleum Augustus
built for himself and his family. Next to it is an
unattractive modern edifice that shelters the
(45) Ara Pacis (Altar of Augustan Peace), erected in
13 BC to celebrate the era of peace ushered in by
Augustus's military victories. The reliefs on the
marble enclosure are magnificent. *Via Ripetta,
tel. 06/671–0271. Admission: 3,750 lire. Open
May–Sept., Wed.–Fri. 9–1:30, Tues. and
Thurs. 9–1:30 and 4–7, Sun. 9–1; Oct.–Apr.,
Tues.–Sat. 9–1:30, Sun. 9–1.*

The Jewish Ghetto and Trastevere

For the authentic atmosphere of Old Rome, explore the old Jewish ghetto and the narrow
streets of Trastevere, two tightly knit communi-
ties whose inhabitants proudly claim descent—
whether real or imagined—from the ancient Romans. Then climb the Janiculum, a hill with
views over the whole city, a vantage point be-
loved of all Romans.

The shadowy area bounded by Piazza Campitelli
and Lungotevere Cenci constituted Rome's old
Jewish ghetto. Within this cramped quarter,
until 1870, all Rome's Jews (and they were
many, tracing their presence in the city to ancient Roman times) were confined under a rigid
all-night curfew. At the little church opposite
Quattro Capi bridge, they were forced to attend
sermons that aimed to convert them to Catholi-
cism, and to pay for the privilege.

Many Jews have remained here, close to the
(46) bronze-roofed **synagogue** on Lungotevere Cenci
and to the roots of their community. Among the
most interesting sights in the ghetto are the
(47) pretty **Fontana delle Tartarughe** (Turtle Fountain) on Piazza Mattei; the old houses on Via
Portico d'Ottavia, where medieval inscriptions
and ancient friezes testify to the venerable age
of these buildings; and the **Teatro di Marcello,**
hardly recognizable as a theater now, but built

at the end of the 1st century BC by Julius Caesar
to hold 20,000 spectators.

Time Out Stop to indulge in American and Austrian baked
goods at **Dolceroma** (Via Portico d'Ottavia 20/b.
Closed Sun. afternoon and Mon.).

---

(48) Cross the Tiber over the ancient Ponte Fabricio
to the **Tiberina Island,** where a city hospital
stands on a site that has been dedicated to heal-
ing ever since a temple to Aesculapius was
erected here in 291 BC. If you have time, and if
the river's not too high, go down the stairs for a
different perspective on the island and the
Tiber, which has begun to undermine the island
in recent years, threatening its structures.

Then continue across Ponte Cestio into
Trastevere, a maze of narrow streets that, despite creeping gentrification, is still one of the
city's most authentically Roman neighborhoods
(for another, explore the jumble of streets between the Roman Forum, Santa Maria Maggiore, and the Colosseum). Among self-consciously
picturesque trattorias and trendy tearooms,
you'll also find old shops in alleys festooned with
washing hung out to dry and dusty artisans'
workshops. Trastevere's population has become
increasingly diverse, and it has acquired a repu-
tation for purse-snatching and petty thievery,
so keep purses and cameras out of sight as you
(49) stroll these byways. Be sure to see **Piazza Santa
Maria in Trastevere,** the heart of the quarter,
with one of Rome's oldest churches, decorated
inside and out with 12th- and 13th-century mosaics.

Follow Via della Scala to Via della Lungara,
where Raphael decorated the garden loggia of
(50) **Villa Farnesina** for extravagant host Agostino
Chigi, who delighted in impressing guests by
having his servants clear the table by casting
precious gold and silver dinnerware into the
Tiber. Naturally, the guests did not know he
had nets stretched under the water to catch
everything. *Via della Lungara 230, tel. 06/654–
0565. Admission free. Open Mon.–Sat. 9–1.*

From Porta Settimiana you can follow Via Garibaldi as it curves up to the Janiculum, past the

⑤¹ church of **San Pietro in Montorio,** known for its
views and for the Tempietto, Bramante's little
temple in the cloister. Beyond the impressive
Acqua Paola Fountain, you'll come upon the **Janiculum Park,** which offers splendid views of
Rome.

The Catacombs and the Appian Way

This tour offers a respite from museums, though
it's no easier on the feet. Do it on a sunny day
and take along a picnic or have lunch at one of
the pleasant restaurants near the catacombs.
The Rome EPT office offers a free, informative
pamphlet on this itinerary. Take Bus 118 from
San Giovanni in Laterano to the **Via Appia
Antica** ("the Queen of Roads"), completed in 312
BC by Appius Claudius, who also built Rome's
first aqueduct. (Stay on the bus until you reach
the catacombs; the most interesting walk along
the ancient road lies beyond them.) You pass
Porta San Sebastiano, which gives you a good
idea of what the city's 5th-century fortifications
looked like, and farther along you'll see the little
church of **Domine Quo Vadis,** where tradition
says that Christ appeared to St. Peter, inspir-
ing him to return to Rome to face martyrdom.

There are two important **catacombs** on the Via
Appia Antica. The first you come upon is that of
San Callisto, one of the best preserved of these
underground cemeteries. A friar will guide you
through its crypts and galleries. *Via Appia
Antica 110, tel. 06/513–6725. Admission: 6,000
lire. Open Apr.–Sept., Thurs.–Tues. 8:30–
noon, 2:30–5:30; Oct.–Mar., Thurs.–Tues.
8:30–noon, 2:30–5.*

The 4th-century catacomb of **San Sebastiano,** a
little farther on, which was named for the saint
who was buried here, burrows underground on
four levels. The only one of the catacombs to remain accessible during the Middle Ages, it is the
origin of the term "catacomb," for it was located
in a spot where the road dips into a hollow, a
place the Romans called *catacumbas* (near the
hollow). Eventually, the Christian cemetery
that had existed here since the 2nd century
came to be known by the same name, which was
applied to all underground cemeteries discov-

ered in Rome in later centuries. *Via Appia Antica 136, tel. 06/788–7035. Admission: 6,000 lire. Open Fri.–Wed. 9–noon and 2:30–5.*

On the other side of Via Appia Antica are the ruins of the **Circus of Maxentius,** where the obelisk now in Piazza Navona once stood. Farther along is the circular **Tomb of Cecilia Metella,** mausoleum of a Roman noblewoman who lived at the time of Julius Caesar. It was transformed into a fortress in the 14th century.

Time Out | There are several trattorias along the Via Appia Antica, most of them moderately priced (*see* Chapter 5, Dining). For a sandwich or a snack, the bar on the corner of Via Appia Antica and Via Cecilia Metella, just beyond the tomb, can provide sustenance and a relaxing pause in the adjoining garden.

The Tomb of Cecilia Metella marks the beginning of the most interesting and evocative stretch of the Via Appia Antica, lined with tombs and fragments of statuary. Cypresses and umbrella pines stand guard over the ruined sepulchers, and the occasional tracts of ancient paving stones are the same ones trod by triumphant Roman legions.

Rome for Free

Most of Rome's sights are either inexpensive or, more commonly, free of charge. You could construct several memorable itineraries devoted exclusively to architecture and religious art—taking in dozens of piazzas, churches, streets, and fountains—and not part with a single lira. Museums and galleries, of course, usually do charge admission, but it's rarely steep, and there are some surprising exceptions, such as the following:

The Colosseum—Lower Level (Ancient Rome).
The Tombs of the Popes (The Vatican).
The Vatican Museums on the Last Sunday of the Month (The Vatican Museums).
The Pantheon (Old Rome).
Villa Farnesina (The Jewish Ghetto and Trastevere).

What to See and Do with Children

Take children to a **pizzeria** with a wood-burning oven, where they can see the chef work with the dough. Take a ride in a **horse and carriage**—it's fun and feels a lot less silly than it looks. Climb or take the elevator to the roof of **St. Peter's**—and look down on the main altar from above. Spend some time in the **Villa Borghese,** perhaps taking in a **Punch and Judy show** on the Pincio. There's another Punch and Judy show on the **Janiculum** hill, where there is also a colorful stand selling puppets.

In December and early January, visit the big **Christmas bazaar** at Piazza Navona, then stop at the huge toy store at the north end of the square. For an almost comical display of orchestration, pause awhile to watch the policeman directing traffic from his little podium in the middle of **Piazza Venezia.** A small-scale but completely serious spectacle is the daily **changing of the guard** at the Quirinale Palace, the residence of the president of Italy. Every day at 4 PM there's a military band and parade as the guards change shifts.

Rome's residential EUR (Esposizone Universal Roma; begun in the late 1930s as a site of a World's Fair that never happened because of World War II) suburb is the home of the well-run **Luna Park** amusement center, which has a big Ferris wheel, a roller coaster, and other rides and games. It can be reached by bus No. 707 from San Paolo fuori le Mura. *Via delle Tre Fontane, tel. 06/592–5933. Admission free, but you pay for each ride. Closed Tues.*

There's usually a **circus** somewhere in town: Check billboards and newspaper listings. Also check listings for cartoon films at the movies and for puppet shows and other children's programs at theaters.

Explore **Castel Sant'Angelo** (*see* The Vatican, *above*). It's got dungeons, battlements, cannons, and cannonballs, and a collection of antique weapons and armor.

Rent **bicycles** and ride around Villa Borghese and the center of town on Sunday, when the traffic is lighter.

Off the Beaten Track

Stroll through the quiet, green neighborhood of the **Aventine Hill,** one of the seven hills of ancient Rome that most tourists don't see. It has several of the city's oldest and least-visited churches, as well as a delightful surprise: the view from the keyhole in the gate to the garden of the Knights of Malta (Piazza Cavalieri di Malta).

Visit the excavations under St. Peter's for a fascinating glimpse of the underpinnings of the great basilica, which was built over the cemetery where archaeologists say they have found **St. Peter's tomb.** *Apply a few days in advance (or try in the morning for the same day) to the* Ufficio Scavi (Excavations Office), to the right beyond the Arco delle Campane entrance to the Vatican, which is left of the basilica. Just tell the Swiss guard you want the Ufficio Scavi, and he will let you by. Tel. 06/698–5318. Admission: 10,000 lire with guide, 6,000 lire with taped guide. Ufficio Scavi open Mon.–Sat. 9–5.

See the **Protestant Cemetery** behind the Piramide, a stone pyramid built in 12 BC at the order of the Roman praetor (senior magistrate) who was buried there. The cemetery is reminiscent of a country churchyard. Among the headstones you'll find Keats's tomb and the place where Shelley's heart was buried. *Via Caio Cestio 6, tel. 06/574–1141. Ring for the custodian. An offering of 500–1,000 lire is customary. Open daily 8–11:30 and 3:20–5:30.*

Explore the subterranean dwellings under the church of **San Clemente.** *Via San Giovanni in Laterano, tel. 06/704–51018. Donation requested. Open Mon.–Sat. 9–noon and 3:30–6, Sun. 10–noon.*

Have an inexpensive lunch at **L'Eau Vive,** run by lay Catholic missionary workers. Though it's elegant and fairly expensive for an evening meal, the good fixed-price lunch is a bargain. *Via*

Monterone 85 (off Piazza Sant'Eustachio), tel. 06/654–1095. AE, DC, V. Closed Sun. Or join the Romans who lunch downstairs at the **Savoy Hotel's** reasonably priced self-service buffet. *Via Ludovisi 15 (the glass door next to the main entrance). Open for lunch only. Closed Sun.*

Sports

Participant Sports

Biking You can rent a bike at Via di Porta Castello 43 (tel. 06/687–5714) and at Piazza Navona 69. There are rental concessions at the Piazza di Spagna and Piazza del Popolo metro stops, at Largo San Silvestro, Largo Argentina, Viale della Pineta in Villa Borghese, and at Viale del Bambino on the Pincio.

Bowling There's a large American-style bowling center, **Bowling Brunswick** (Lungotevere Acqua Acetosa, tel. 06/808–6147), and a smaller one, **Bowling Roma** (Viale Regina Margherita 181, tel. 06/855–1184).

Fitness Facilities The **Cavalieri Hilton** (Via Cadlolo 101, tel. 06/31511) offers a 600-meter jogging path on the hotel grounds as well as an outdoor pool, two clay tennis courts, an exercise area, a sauna, and a steam room. The **Sheraton Roma** (Viale del Pattinaggio, tel. 06/5453) has a heated outdoor pool, a tennis court, two squash courts, and a sauna, but no gym. The **Sheraton Golf** (Viale Parco de' Medici 22, tel. 06/659788) has a fitness center and golf course. The **St. Peter's Holiday Inn** (Via Aurelia Antica 415, tel. 06/6642) has two tennis courts on the hotel grounds. It also has a 25-meter outdoor pool.

The **Roman Sport Center** (Via del Galoppatoio 33, tel. 06/320–1667) is a vast sports center next to the underground parking lot in Villa Borghese; it has two swimming pools, a gym, aerobic workout areas, squash courts, and saunas. It is affiliated with the **American Health Club** (Largo Somalia 60, tel. 06/862–12411).

Golf The oldest and most prestigious golf club in Rome is the **Circolo del Golf Roma** (Via Acqua Santa 3, tel. 06/784–3079). The newest are the

Sheraton Golf course (Viale Parco de' Medici 22, tel. 06/655–3477 for clubhouse) and the Country Club Castel Gandolfo (Via Santo Spirito 13, Castel Gandolfo, tel. 06/931–2301). The Golf Club Fioranello (Viale della Repubblica, tel. 06/713–8212) is at Santa Maria delle Mole, off the Via Appia Antica. There is an 18-hole course at the Olgiata Golf Club (Largo Olgiata 15, on the Via Cassia, tel. 06/378–9141). Nonmembers are welcome in these clubs but must show membership cards of their home golf or country clubs.

Horseback Riding There are several riding clubs in Rome. The most central is the Associazione Sportiva Villa Borghese (Via del Galoppatoio 23, tel. 06/360–6797). You can also ride at the Società Ippica Romana (Via Monti della Farnesina 18, tel. 06/396–6214) and at the Circolo Ippico Olgiata (Largo Olgiata 15, tel. 06/378–8792), outside the city on the Via Cassia.

Jogging The best bet for jogging in the inner city is the Villa Borghese. A circuit of the Pincio, among the marble statuary, measures half a mile. A longer run in the park itself might include a loop around Piazza di Siena, a grass horse track measuring a quarter of a mile. Although most traffic is barred from Villa Borghese, government and police cars sometimes speed through. Be careful to stick to the sides of the roads. For a long run away from all traffic, try Villa Ada and Villa Doria Pamphili on the Janiculum. On the other hand, if you really love history, jog at the old Circus Maximus, or along Via delle Terme di Caracalla, which is flanked by a park. (Also, *see* The Cavalieri Hilton in Fitness Facilities, *above*.)

Swimming The outdoor pools of the Cavalieri Hilton (Via Cadlolo 101, tel. 06/31511) and the Hotel Aldovrandi (Via Ulisse Aldovrandi 15, tel. 06/322–3993) are lush summer oases open to nonguests. The Roman Sport Center (Via del Galoppatoio 33, tel. 06/320–1667) has two swimming pools, and there's another one at the American Health Club (Largo Somalia 60, tel. 06/862–12411).

Tennis Increasingly popular with Italians, tennis is played in private clubs and on many public courts that can be rented by the hour. Your hotel *portiere* will direct you to the nearest courts and can book for you. A prestigious Roman club is the **Tennis Club Parioli** (Largo de Morpurgo 2, Via Salaria, tel. 06/862–00882).

Spectator Sports

Basketball   Basketball continues to grow in popularity in Italy, with many American pros now playing on Italian teams. In Rome, games are played at the **Palazzo dello Sport** in the EUR district (Piazzale dello Sport, tel. 06/592–5107).

Horseback Riding   The **International Riding Show,** held the last few days of April and the first week in May, draws a stylish crowd to the amphitheater of Piazza di Siena in Villa Borghese. The competition is stiff, and the program features a cavalry charge staged by the dashing mounted corps of the *carabinieri.* For information, call the **Italian Federation of Equestrian Sports** (Viale Tiziano 70, tel. 06/323–3806).

Horse Racing   There's flat racing at the lovely century-old **Capannelle** track (Via Appia Nuova 1255, tel. 06/718–3143), frequented by a chic crowd on big race days. The trotters meet at the **Tor di Valle** track (Via del Mare, tel. 06/529–0269).

Soccer   Italy's favorite spectator sport stirs passionate enthusiasm among partisans. Games are usually held on Sunday afternoon throughout the fall–spring season. Roma and Lazio play their home games in the Olympic Stadium at **Foro Italico.** Tickets are on sale at the box office before the games; your hotel portiere may be able to help you get tickets in advance. The Olympic Stadium is on Viale dei Gladiatori, in the extensive Foro Italico sports complex built by Mussolini on the banks of the Tiber (tel. 06/333–6316).

Tennis   A top-level international tournament is held at the Tennis Stadium at **Foro Italico** in May. For information, call the **Italian Tennis Federation** (Viale Tiziano 70, tel. 06/368–58510).

Beaches

The beaches nearest Rome are at **Ostia,** a busy urban center in its own right; **Castelfusano,** nearby; **Fregene,** a villa colony; and **Castelporziano,** a public beach area maintained by the

city. At Ostia and Fregene, you pay for changing cabins, cabanas, umbrellas, and such, and
for the fact that the sand is kept clean and
combed. Some establishments, such as **Kursaal**
(Lungomare Catullo 36 at Castelfusano, tel. 06/
562–1303) have swimming pools, strongly recommended as alternatives to the notoriously
polluted waters of the Mediterranean. You can
reach Ostia by train from Ostiense Station,
Castelfusano and Castelporziano by bus from
Ostia, and Fregene by COTRAL bus from the
Via Lepanto stop of Metro Line A in Rome. All
beaches are crowded during July and August.

For cleaner water and more of a resort atmosphere, you have to go farther afield. To the
north of Rome, **Santa Marinella** and **Santa
Severa** offer shoals, sand, and attractive sur-
roundings. To the south, **Sabaudia** is known for
miles of sandy beaches, **San Felice Circeo** is a
classy resort, and **Sperlonga** is a picturesque old
town flanked by beaches and pretty coves.

Excursion 1: Ostia Antica

One of the easiest excursions from the capital
takes you west to the sea, where tall pines stand
among the well-preserved ruins of Ostia Antica,
the main port of ancient Rome. Founded around
the 4th century BC, Ostia Antica conveys the
same impression as Pompeii, but on a smaller
scale and in a prettier, parklike setting. The city
was inhabited by rich businessmen, wily merchants, sailors, and slaves. The great *horrea*
(warehouses) were built in the 2nd century AD to
handle huge shipments of grain from Africa; the
insulae, forerunners of the modern apartment
building, provided housing for the growing population. Under the combined assaults of the barbarians and the anopheles mosquito, the port
was eventually abandoned, and it silted up. Tid-
al mud and windblown sand covered the city,
which lay buried until the beginning of this century. Now extensively excavated and excellent-
ly maintained, it makes for a fascinating visit on
a sunny day.

Tourist Information

The admission charge to the **Ostia Antica** excavations includes entrance to the Ostiense Museum, which is on the grounds and observes the same opening hours. *Via dei Romagnoli, tel. 06/565–1405. Admission: 8,000 lire. Open daily 9–one hour before sunset.*

Getting Around

By Car The Via del Mare leads directly from Rome to Ostia Antica; the ride takes about 35 minutes.

By Train There is regular train service from Ostiense train station, near Porta San Paolo, which is connected with the Piramide stop on Metro Line B. Trains leave every half-hour, and the ride takes about 30 minutes.

Exploring

Numbers in the margin correspond to points of interest on the Rome Environs map.

Near the entrance to the *scavi* (excavations) is a fortress built in the 15th century for Pope Julius II. The hamlet that grew up around it is charming. However, your visit to **Ostia Antica** itself starts at **Via delle Tombe,** lined with sepulchers from various periods. From here, passing through the **Porta Romana,** one of the city's three gates, you come to the **Decumanus Maximus,** the main thoroughfare crossing the city from end to end.

About 300 yards up on the right are the **Terme di Nettuno** (Baths of Neptune), decorated with black-and-white mosaics representing Neptune and Amphitrite. Directly behind the baths is the barracks of the fire department, which played an important role in a town with warehouses full of valuable goods and foodstuffs.

Just ahead, and also on the right side of the Decumanus Maximus, is the beautiful **Theater,** built by Augustus and completely restored by Septimius Severus in the 2nd century AD. Behind it, in the vast Piazzale delle Corporazioni, where trade organizations similar to guilds had their offices, is the **Temple of Ceres:** This is appropriate for a town dealing in grain imports,

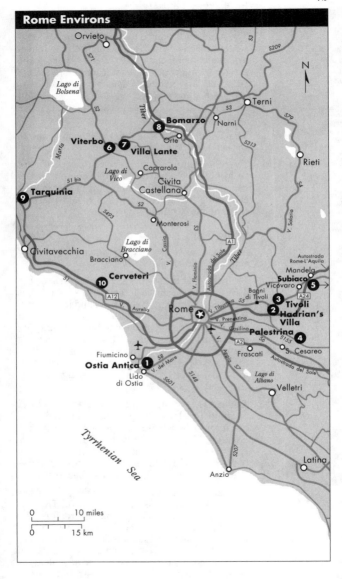

Rome Environs

Orvieto

Lago di Bolsena

S71

S2

Marta

Tiber

Terni

S3

S209

S3

Bomarzo 8

Narni

S313

Viterbo 6 7 **Villa Lante**

Caprarola

Rieti

Lago di Vico

V. Salaria

S1 bis

Civita Castellana

Tarquinia 9

S493

S2

S3

Monterosi

Cassia

A1

Lago di Bracciano

Civitavecchia

Bracciano

S1

V. Flaminia

Autostrada del Sole

Tiber

Autostrada Rome–L'Aquila

Cerveteri 10

A12

Aurelia

V.

V. Tiburtina

Rome

Bagni di Tivoli

Subiaco

Vicovaro

Mandela

5

3 **Tivoli**

2 **Hadrian's Villa**

A24

V. Prenestina

Casilina

Palestrina 4

Fiumicino

Ostia Antica 1

Lido di Ostia

S8

V. del Mare

V. Appia

S148

A2

Frascati

S6

S155

S. Cesareo

Autostrada del Sole

Lago di Albano

Velletri

S601

S207

Latina

Anzio

Tyrrhenian Sea

N

0   10 miles

0   15 km

since Ceres, who gave her name to cereal, was the goddess of agriculture. Next to the theater, where there is a coffee bar, you can visit the **House of Apuleius,** built in Pompeiian style— containing fewer windows, and built lower, than those in Ostia. Next to it is the **Mithraeum,** with balconies and a hall decorated with symbols of the cult of Mithras. This men-only religion, imported from Persia, was especially popular with legionnaires.

On Via dei Molini, 200 yards beyond the theater, there is a mill, where grain for the warehouses next door was ground with the stones you see there. Along Via di Diana, a left turn 50 yards up Via dei Molini, you'll come upon a **thermopolium** (bar) with a marble counter and a fresco depicting the fruit and foodstuffs that were sold here. Turn right at the end of Via di Diana onto Via dei Dipinti; at the end is the **Museo Ostiense,** which displays some of the ancient sculptures and mosaics found among the ruins.

Retrace your steps along Via dei Dipinti and turn right just before Via di Diana for the **Forum,** with monumental remains of the city's most important temple, dedicated to Jupiter, Juno, and Minerva; other ruins of baths; a basilica (in Roman times a basilica served as a secular hall of justice); and smaller temples.

A continuation of the Decumanus Maximus leads from the Forum. From the crossroads, about 100 yards on, Via Epagathiana, on the right, leads down toward the Tiber, where there are large warehouses that were erected in the 2nd century AD to deal with enormous amounts of grain imported into Rome during that period, the height of the Empire.

Take the street opposite the entrance to the warehouses to the **House of Cupid and Psyche,** a residential house named for a statue found there; you can see what remains of a large pool in an enclosed garden decorated with marble and mosaic motifs. It takes little imagination to notice that even in ancient times a premium was placed on water views: The house faces the shore, which would have been only about ¼ mile away. Take Via del Tempio di Ercole left and then go right on Via della Foce to see (on the left) the **House of Serapis,** a 2nd-century multi-level dwelling, and the **Baths of the Seven Wise Men,** named for a fresco found there.

Take Via del Tempio di Serapide away from Via della Foce and then the Cardo Degli Aurighi, where you'll pass—just up on the left—another apartment building. The road leads back to the Decumanus Maximus, which continues to the **Porta Marina.** Off to the left, on what used to be the seashore, are the ruins of the **Synagogue,** one of the oldest in the Western world. This is where you begin your return; Porta Marina is the farthest point in the tour. Go right at the **Bivio del Castrum,** past the slaughterhouse and the large round temple. You'll come to the **Cardine Massimo,** a road lined with ruined buildings. From here, turn left onto Via Semita dei Cippi to see the **House of Fortuna Annonaria,** the richly decorated house of a wealthy Ostian. This is another place to marvel at the skill of the mosaic artists and, at the same time, to realize that this really was someone's home. One of the rooms opens onto a secluded garden.

Continue on Via Semita dei Cippi for about 150 yards until you turn right onto the Decumanus Maximus to retrace the last leg of the tour back to the entrance.

Excursion 2: Tivoli, Palestrina, Subiaco

East of Rome lie some of the region's star attractions, which could be combined along a route that loops through the hills where ancient Romans built their summer resorts. The biggest attraction is Tivoli, which could be seen on a half-day excursion from Rome. But if you continue eastward to Palestrina, you can see a vast sanctuary famous in ancient times. And you could also fit in a visit to the site on which St. Benedict founded the hermitage that gave rise to Western monasticism. The monastery of St. Benedict is in Subiaco—not easy to get to unless you have a car, but you may want to make the effort to gain an insight into medieval mysticism.

Tourist Information

Tivoli (Largo Garibaldi, tel. 0774/293522).
Subiaco (Via Cadorna 59, tel. 0774/85397).

Escorted Tours

American Express (tel. 06/67641) and **CIT** (tel. 06/47941) have half-day excursions to Villa d'Este in Tivoli. **Appian Line** (tel. 06/488–4151) and **Carrani Tours** (tel. 06/482–4194) have morning tours that include Hadrian's Villa.

Getting Around

By Car For Tivoli, take the Via Tiburtina or the Rome–L'Aquila autostrada (A24). From Tivoli to Palestrina, follow signs for the Via Prenestina and Palestrina. To get to Palestrina directly from Rome, take either the Via Prenestina or Via Casilina or take the Autostrada del Sole (A2) to the San Cesareo exit and follow signs for Palestrina; this trip takes about one hour. To get to Subiaco from either Tivoli or Palestrina or directly from Rome, take the autostrada for L'Aquila (A24) to the Vicovaro-Mandela exit, then follow the local road to Subiaco; from Rome, the ride takes about one hour.

By Train The FS train from Termini Station to Palestrina takes about 40 minutes; you can then board a bus from the train station to the center of town.

By Bus COTRAL buses leave for Tivoli every 15 minutes from the terminal at the Rebibbia stop on Metro Line B, but not all take the route that passes near Hadrian's Villa. Inquire which bus passes closest to Villa Adriana and tell the driver to let you off there. The ride takes about 60 minutes. For Palestrina, take the COTRAL bus from the Anagnina stop on Metro Line A. There is local bus service between Tivoli and Palestrina, but check schedules locally. From Rome to Subiaco, take the COTRAL bus from the Rebibbia stop on Metro Line B; buses leave every 40 minutes and those that take the autostrada make the trip in 70 minutes, as opposed to an hour and 45 minutes by another route.

Exploring

Numbers in the margin correspond to points of interest on the Rome Environs map.

The road east from Rome to Tivoli passes through some unattractive industrial areas and burgeoning suburbs. You'll know you're close when you see vast quarries of travertine marble and smell the sulphurous vapors of the little spa, Bagni di Tivoli. This was once green countryside; now it's ugly and overbuilt. But don't despair, because this tour takes you to two of the Rome area's most attractive sights: Hadrian's Villa and the Villa d'Este. The Villa d'Este is popular; fewer people go to Hadrian's Villa. Both are outdoor sights, which entail a lot of walking, and in the case of the Villa D'Este, stair climbing. That also means that good weather is a virtual prerequisite for enjoying the itinerary.

❷ Visit **Hadrian's Villa** first, especially in the summer, to take advantage of the cooler morning sun: There's little shade. Hadrian, who succeeded Trajan as emperor in AD 117, was a man of genius and intellectual curiosity. Fascinated by the accomplishments of the Hellenistic world, he decided to re-create it for his own enjoyment by building this villa over a vast tract of land below the ancient settlement of Tibur. From AD 118 to 130, architects, laborers, and artists worked on the villa, periodically spurred on by the emperor himself, as he returned from another voyage full of ideas for even more daring constructions. After his death in AD 138, the fortunes of his villa declined. It was sacked by barbarians and Romans alike; by the Renaissance, many of his statues and decorations had ended up in the Villa d'Este. Still, it is an impressive complex.

Study the exhibits in the visitors' center at the entrance and the scale model in the building adjacent to the bar, close by. They will increase your enjoyment of the villa by helping you make sense out of what can otherwise be a maze of ruins. It's not the single elements, but the peaceful and harmonious effect of the whole, that makes Hadrian's Villa such a treat. Oleanders, pines, and cypresses growing among the ruins heighten the visual impact. *Villa Adriana. Admission: 8,000 lire. Open daily 9 AM–90 min before sunset.*

Time Out   The **Adriano** restaurant, at the entrance to Hadrian's Villa, is a handy place to have lunch and to rest before heading up the hill to the Villa d'Este. The food is good, the cost moderate, and the atmosphere relaxing. (Closed Mon.)

From Hadrian's Villa, catch the local bus up to **❸ Tivoli**'s main square, Largo Garibaldi. Take a left onto Via Boselli and cross Piazza Trento, with the church of Santa Maria Maggiore on your left, to reach the entrance to the **Villa d'Este.** Ippolito d'Este was an active figure in the political intrigues of mid-16th-century Italy. He was also a cardinal, thanks to his grandfather, Alexander VI, the infamous Borgia pope. To console himself at a time when he saw his political star in decline, Ippolito tore down part of a Franciscan monastery that occupied the site he had chosen for his villa. Then the determined prelate diverted the Aniene River into a channel to run under the town and provide water for the Villa d'Este's fountains. Big, small, noisy, quiet, rushing, and running, the fountains create a late-Renaissance playground, which is now, sadly, run down, with fountains halfheartedly spouting polluted water. *Villa d'Este. Admission: 5,000 lire. Open daily 9–90 min before sunset.*

Only 27 kilometers (17 miles) south of Tivoli on S636 and 37 kilometers (23 miles) outside Rome **❹** along Via Prenestina, **Palestrina** is set on the slopes of Mount Ginestro, from which it commands a sweeping view of the green plain and distant mountains. It is surprisingly little known outside Italy, except to students of ancient history and music lovers. Its most famous native son, Giovanni Pierluigi da Palestrina, born here in 1525, was the renowned composer of 105 masses, as well as madrigals, magnificats, and motets. But the town was celebrated long before the composer's lifetime.

Ancient Praeneste, modern Palestrina, was founded much earlier than Rome. It was the site of the Temple of Fortuna Primigenia, which dates from the beginning of the 2nd century BC. This was one of the biggest, richest, and most frequented temple complexes in all antiquity. People came from far and wide to consult its famous oracle, yet in modern times, no one had any idea of the extent of the complex until World War II bombings exposed ancient foundations that stretched way out into the plain below the town. It has since become clear that the temple area was larger than the town of Palestrina is today. Now you can make out the four superimposed terraces that formed the main part of the temple; they were built up on great arches and were linked by broad flights of stairs. The whole town sits on top of what was once the main part of the temple.

Large arches and terraces scale the hillside up to the **Palazzo Barberini,** built in the 17th century along the semicircular lines of the original temple. It's now a museum containing a wealth of material found on the site, some dating back to the 4th century BC. The collection of splendid engraved bronze urns was plundered by art thieves in 1991, but they couldn't carry off the chief attraction, a 1st-century BC mosaic representing the Nile in flood. This delightful work—a large-scale composition in which form, color, and innumerable details captivate the eye—is alone worth the trip to Palestrina. But there's more: a model of the temple as it was in ancient times, which will help you appreciate the immensity of the original construction. *Museo Nazionale Archeologico, Palazzo Barberini. Admission: 6,000 lire. Open Tues.– Sun., spring and fall 9–6, summer 9–7:30, winter 9–4.*

If you are driving or if you don't mind setting out on a roundabout route by local bus, you could **5** continue on to **Subiaco,** tucked away in the mountains above Tivoli and Palestrina. Take S155 east for about 40 kilometers (25 miles) before turning left onto S411 for the remaining 25 kilometers (15 miles) to Subiaco. Its inaccessibility was undoubtedly a point in its favor for St. Benedict: The 6th-century monastery that he founded here became a landmark of Western monasticism.

This excursion is best made by car because it's nearly a 3-kilometer (2-mile) walk from Subiaco to Santa Scolastica, and another half-hour by footpath up to San Benedetto. If you don't have a car, inquire in Subiaco about a local bus to get you at least part of the way.

The first monastery you come upon is that of **Santa Scolastica,** actually a convent, and the only one of the hermitages founded by St. Benedict and his sister Scholastica to have survived the Lombard invasion of Italy in the 9th century. It has three cloisters, the oldest dating back to the 13th century. The library, which is not open to visitors, contains some precious volumes; this was the site of the first print shop in Italy, set up in 1474. *Admission free. Open daily 9–12:30, 4–7.*

Drive up to the **monastery of St. Benedict,** or take the footpath that climbs the hill. The monastery was built over the grotto where St. Benedict lived and meditated. Clinging to the cliff on nine great arches, it has resisted the assaults of man and nature for almost 800 years. You climb a broad, sloping avenue and enter through a little wooden veranda, where a Latin inscription augurs "peace to those who enter." You find yourself in the colorful world of the upper church, every inch of it covered with frescoes by Umbrian and Sienese artists of the 14th century. In front of the main altar, a stairway leads down to the lower church, carved out of the rock, with yet another stairway down to the grotto, or cave, where St. Benedict lived as a hermit for three years. The frescoes here are even earlier than those above; look for the portrait of St. Francis of Assisi, painted from life in 1210, in the Chapel of St. Gregory, and for the oldest fresco in the monastery, in the Shepherd's Grotto. *Admission free. Open daily 9–12:30, 3–6.*

Back in town, if you've got the time, stop at the 14th-century **church of San Francesco** to see the frescoes by Il Sodoma. *Ring for admission.*

Excursion 3: Viterbo, Cerveteri, Tuscia

Scattered throughout the undulating countryside northwest of Rome are ancient Etruscan sites, medieval towns, and grandiose Renaissance villas. The attractions of this part of the region are not as well known as Tivoli or Ostia Antica, and they offer the promise of discovery. If you do not have a car, however, it takes some planning and determination to plot out an itinerary by bus or train that takes in more than one place at a time. If you are using public transportation you may want to limit your forays to an excursion from Rome to Viterbo and another from Rome to Cerveteri. Touring by car allows you to take in Lake Bracciano and its massive 15th-century castle, the imposing Palazzo Farnese at Caprarola, and the eccentric stone sculptures in the so-called Monster Park of Bomarzo, the folly of a Renaissance prince.

The area now known as Tuscia was Etruria, heartland of the Etruscan civilization that flourished here for almost one thousand years before it was overcome and assimilated by ancient Rome. To learn more about the Etruscans, read D. H. Lawrence's *Etruscan Places* (1932), and take in some of the collections of Etruscan art and artifacts in the Museum of Villa Giulia in Rome. Then visit Cerveteri and, if possible, Tarquinia and some of the other Etruscan sites. No homework is necessary to appreciate the charm of the walled city of Viterbo, capital of Tuscia. Viterbo's medieval quarter is well preserved and artlessly picturesque—a neighborhood where everyday life goes on in a 12th-century setting.

Tuscia's dramatically beautiful landscape hints at mystery. The rolling farmland is punctuated by forested hills and scarred by gorges where thick underbrush conceals shallow streams running swiftly in dark, rocky beds. Scenic roads trace the rims of extinct volcano craters, now receptacles of the deep waters of lakes Bracciano, Vico, and Bolsena. A drive through Tuscia holds the promise of some singular sights.

Tourist Information

Bracciano (Via Claudia 58, tel. 06/998–6782).
Cerveteri (Ladispoli, Via Duca degli Abruzzi 147, tel. 06/991–3049).
Tarquinia (Piazza Cavour 1, tel. 0766/856384).
Viterbo (Piazzale dei Caduti 14, tel. 0761/234795).

Getting Around

By Car   This is the best way to see the area. From Rome, take Via Cassia (S2) to Monterosi, then turn off onto Via Cimina, a scenic road along the rim of the volcanic crater that now forms Lake Vico; you can detour east off Via Cimina to Caprarola to see the Palazzo Farnese before continuing on Via Cimina to Viterbo. If you leave Rome by way of Via Claudia (S493) you can detour to Lake Bracciano and visit the castle of Bracciano; you will also pass several Etruscan sites, including San Giuliano and Blera, before reaching Viterbo. The drive (either route) takes from 75 to 90 minutes, not counting detours for sightseeing. Another fast way to Viterbo is via Autostrada A1 to Orte, where you exit and take the Orte–Viterbo Raccordo, an expressway. Or you can stay on the Autostrada until the Attigliano exit, which is about 3 miles from Bomarzo and the Monster Park, then press on from Bomarzo via the Orte–Viterbo Raccordo. By autostrada the trip to Viterbo takes from 40 minutes to an hour (via Bomarzo).

For Tarquinia, take the Via Cassia southwest from Viterbo and turn off onto S1 bis, which takes you to Via Aurelia (S1), the main coast highway connecting Tarquinia and Cerveteri with Rome. Or drive directly from Rome to Cerveteri on the Rome–Civitavecchia expressway (A12) or Via Aurelia. The ride takes about 40 minutes. For Tarquinia, continue north on S1; the trip takes about 90 minutes.

By Bus   To Viterbo, take the Ferrovia Roma Nord train to the Saxa Rubra stop, where you get the COTRAL bus to Viterbo. The ride takes 60 minutes on an express (*diretto*) bus, 90 minutes on slower buses. To Cerveteri, take the COTRAL bus from Lepanto Station on Metro Line A; the ride takes about 40 minutes. To Tarquinia, take

the COTRAL bus from Lepanto Station on
Metro Line A; the trip takes about 90 minutes.

By Train You can take a Ferrovia Roma Nord train directly to Viterbo, but service is infrequent and the
ride takes about two hours. Local FS trains on
the Rome–Pisa line stop at Ladispoli, where you
may be able to get a bus to Cerveteri, but bus
service is erratic and Cerveteri is 5 miles away.
COTRAL buses from Rome are more direct. On
the same FS line, Tarquinia is about 50 minutes
away by local train, and there are buses from
the station to Tarquinia, about 1 mile uphill.

Exploring

*Numbers in the margin correspond to points of
interest on the Rome Environs map.*

❻ **Viterbo** is about 80 kilometers (50 miles) from
Rome in the heart of Tuscia, the modern name
for the Etruscan domain of Etruria. Viterbo's
chief attractions are its 12th-century walls and
towers, the historic palace of the popes who held
court here in the 13th century, and the perfectly
preserved medieval quarter. At a conclave held
at the **Palazzo Papale** in 1271 to elect a new pope,
the people of Viterbo took a stand that has gone
down in history. The conclave had dragged on
for months, apparently making no progress.
Weary of providing the cardinals with room and
board, the people of Viterbo dismantled the roof
of the conclave hall and put the churchmen on
bread and water. Sure enough, a new pope—
Gregory X—was elected in short order. The
fine Romanesque **cathedral** next to the Papal
Palace has a Renaissance facade. The interior
has been restored to its original medieval style,
but the chipped marble columns owe their look
to a bomb that fell during World War II. To the
left of the cathedral is a fine 15th-century town
house.

Walk down Via San Lorenzo and follow Via San
Pellegrino through the **medieval quarter of San
Pellegrino,** one of the best preserved in Italy.
The old buildings, towers, arches, vaults, and
characteristic exterior staircases are made of
the dark local volcanic stone called *peperino*. At
the end of Via San Pellegrino, turn left toward
Via delle Fabbriche and Piazza della Fontana

So, you're getting away from it all.

Just make sure you can get back.

AT&T Access Numbers
Dial the number of the country you're in to reach AT&T.

*AUSTRIA†††	022-903-011	*GREECE	00-800-1311	NORWAY	800-190-11
*BELGIUM	0-800-100-10	*HUNGARY	00 ◇ -800-01111	POLAND†◆²	0 ◇ 010-480-0111
BULGARIA	00-1800-0010	*ICELAND	999-001	PORTUGAL†	05017-1-288
CANADA	1-800-575-2222	IRELAND	1-800-550-000	ROMANIA	01-800-4288
CROATIA†◆	99-38-0011	ISRAEL	177-100-2727	*RUSSIA† (MOSCOW)	155-5042
*CYPRUS	080-90010	*ITALY	172-1011	SLOVAKIA	00-420-00101
CZECH REPUBLIC	00-420-00101	KENYA†	0800-10	SOUTH AFRICA	0-800-99-0123
*DENMARK	8001-0010	*LIECHTENSTEIN	155-00-11	SPAIN•	900-99-00-11
*EGYPT¹ (CAIRO)	510-0200	LITHUANIA◆	8 ◇ 196	*SWEDEN	020-795-611
*FINLAND	9800-100-10	LUXEMBOURG	0-800-0111	*SWITZERLAND	155-00-11
FRANCE	19 ◇ -0011	F.Y.R. MACEDONIA	99-800-4288	*TURKEY	00-800-12277
*GAMBIA	00111	*MALTA	0800-890-110	UKRAINE†	8 ◇ 100-11
GERMANY	0130-0010	*NETHERLANDS	06-022-9111	UK	0500-89-0011

Countries in bold face permit country-to-country calling in addition to calls to the U.S. **WorldConnect℠** prices consist of **USADirect®** rates plus an additional charge based on the country you are calling. Collect calling available to the U.S. only. *Public phones require deposit of coin or phone card. ◇ Await second dial tone. † May not be available from every phone. ◆ Not available from public phones. ¹Dial "02" first, outside Cairo. ²Dial 010-480-0111 from major Warsaw hotels. • Calling available to most European countries. ©1994 AT&T.

Here's a travel tip that will make it easy to call back to the States. Dial the access number for the country you're in to get English-speaking AT&T operators or voice prompts. Minimize hotel telephone surcharges too.

If all the countries you're visiting aren't listed above, call **1 800 241-5555** for a free wallet card with all AT&T access numbers. Easy international calling from AT&T. **TrueWorld Connections.**

American Express offers Travelers Cheques built for two.

Cheques *for Two*℠ from American Express are the Travelers Cheques that allow either of you to use them because both of you have signed them. And only one of you needs to be present to purchase them.

Cheques *for Two* are accepted anywhere regular American Express Travelers Cheques are, which is just about everywhere. So stop by your bank, AAA* or any American Express Travel Service Office and ask for Cheques *for Two*.

Travelers Cheques

Grande, where the largest and most original of Viterbo's medieval fountains still spouts steady streams of water. From the center of town, take **7** a bus or drive to Bagnaia to see **Villa Lante,** a splendid example of an Italian formal garden, studded with fountains and set in a lush park. *Admission: 5,000 lire. Open Tues.–Sun. 9 AM– one hour before sunset.*

If you have come by car, make a detour to **8** **Bomarzo,** where the Parco dei Mostri (Monster Park) created in the 16th-century for Prince Vicino Orsini is characterized by eccentric architecture populated by surreal sculptures of mythical monsters. *Admission: 10,000 lire. Open daily 9 AM–one hour before sunset.*

Whether you reach Tarquinia and/or Cerveteri from Viterbo or Rome, you will find their necropolises. In these slightly unsettling cities of the dead, the Etruscans laid the deceased to rest, providing them with everything they might need to enjoy the afterlife: food, utensils, pictures, clothing, jewels, and arms. A highlight **9** of a visit to **Tarquinia** is the sight of the marvelous golden terra-cotta horses from a frieze that once decorated an Etruscan temple. This remarkable evidence of the artistic mastery achieved by the Etruscans is mounted in the main hall of the **Etruscan Museum** in Palazzo Vitelleschi. There are also ranks of sarcophagi and other Etruscan artifacts, together with some wall paintings that have been removed from the underground tombs that surround this sleepy provincial town. You can visit some of the underground tombs with a guide and see other paintings. *Admission: 8,000 lire, valid for both museum and necropolis. Open July–Sept., Tues.–Sun. 9–2, 4–7; Oct.–June, Tues.–Sun. 9–2.*

10 At **Cerveteri,** the tombs in the **Banditaccia Necropolis** outside of town are modeled on Etruscan dwellings and decorated with reliefs carved in stone. *Admission: 8,000 lire. Open May–Sept., Tues.–Sun. 9–7; Oct.–Apr., Tues.–Sun. 9–4.*

4 Shopping

Shopping in Rome is part of the fun. You're sure to find something that suits your fancy *and* your pocketbook, but don't expect to get bargains on Italian brands, such as Benetton, that are exported to the United States; prices are about the same on both sides of the Atlantic.

Shops are open from 9 or 9:30 to 1 and from 3:30 or 4 to 7 or 7:30. There's a tendency in Rome for shops in central districts to stay open all day, but for many this is still in the experimental stage. Department stores and centrally located UPIM and Standa stores are open all day. Remember that most stores are closed Sunday and, with the exception of food and technical-supply stores, also on Monday mornings from September to June and Saturday afternoons in July and August. Most Italian sizes are not uniform, so always try on clothing before you buy, or measure gift items. Glove sizes are universal. In any case, remember that Italian stores generally will *not* refund your purchases and that they often cannot exchange goods because of limited stock. *Always* take your purchases with you; having them shipped home from the shop can cause hassles. If circumstances are such that you can't take your goods with you, and if the shop seems reliable about shipping, get a firm statement of *when* and *how* your purchase will be sent.

Prezzi fissi means that prices are fixed, and it's a waste of time bargaining unless you're buying a sizable quantity of goods or a particularly costly object. Most stores have a fixed-price policy, and most honor a variety of credit cards. They will also accept foreign money at the current exchange rate, give or take a few lire. You may need a receipt at customs on your return home. Bargaining is still an art at Porta Portese flea market and is routine when purchasing anything from a street vendor.

IVA (VAT) Refunds Under Italy's IVA-refund system, a non-EU resident can obtain a refund of tax paid after spending a total of 300,000 lire in one store (before tax—and note that price tags and prices quoted, unless otherwise stated, include IVA). Shop with your passport and ask the store for an invoice itemizing the article(s), price(s), and the

86

Rome Shopping

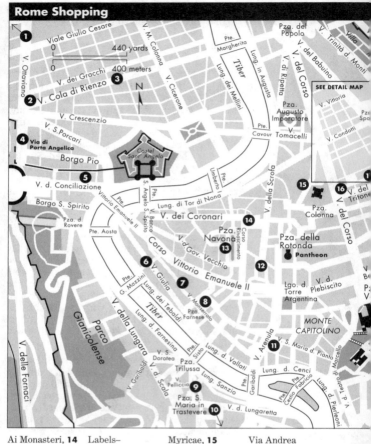

Ai Monasteri, **14**
Campo dei Fiori, **8**
Ceresa, **20**
Cesari, **22**
Cinecittà-Due, **33**
Coin, **31**
Di Cori, **30**
Frugoni, **11**
Galtrucco, **17**

Labels–for–Less, **28**
La Galleria, **9**
Lavori Artigianali Femminili, **19**
Luisa Spagnoli, **26**
Magli, **24**
Meconi, **2**

Myricae, **15**
Nardecchia, **13**
Nickol's, **21**
Porta Portese, **10**
Piazza Vittorio, **32**
Rinascente, **16, 27**
Tanca, **12**

Via Andrea Doria, **1**
Via Cola di Rienzo, **3**
Via della Conciliazione, **5**
Via del Tritone, **18**
Via di Porta Angelica, **4**

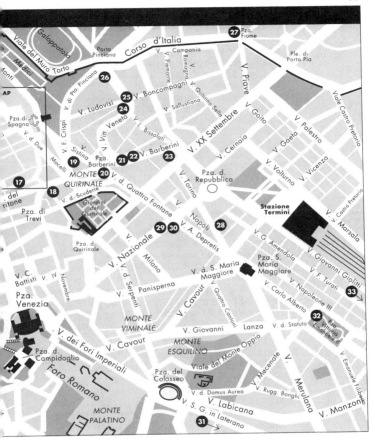

amount of tax. At departure, take the still-unused goods and the invoice to the customs office at the airport or other point of departure and have the invoice stamped. (If you return to the United States or Canada directly from Italy, go through the procedure at Italian customs; if your return is, say, via Britain, take the Italian goods and invoice to British customs.) Once back home—and within 90 days of the date of purchase—mail the stamped invoice to the store, which will forward the IVA rebate to you. A growing number of stores in Rome are members of the Tax-Free Shopping System, which expedites things by providing an invoice that is actually a Tax-Free Cheque in the amount of the refund. Once stamped, it can be cashed at the Tax-Free Cash refund window at major airports and border crossings.

Shopping Districts The most elegant and expensive shops are concentrated in the **Piazza di Spagna** area especially along **Via Condotti** and **Via Borgognona.** **Via Margutta** is known for art galleries and **Via del Babuino** for antiques. There are several high-fashion outlets on **Via Gregoriana** and **Via Sistina.** Bordering this top-price shopping district is **Via del Corso,** which—along with **Via Frattina** and **Via del Gambero**—is lined with shops and boutiques of all kinds.

Via del Tritone, leading up from Piazza Colonna off Via del Corso, has medium-to expensive-priced shops selling everything from fashion fabrics to trendy furniture. Farther up, on **Via Veneto,** you'll find more high-priced boutiques and shoe stores, as well as newsstands selling English-language newspapers, magazines, and paperbacks. **Via Nazionale** features shoe stores, moderately priced boutiques, and shops selling men's and women's fashions. **Via Cola di Rienzo** offers high-quality goods of all types; it's a good alternative to the Piazza di Spagna area.

In Old Rome, **Via dei Coronari** has antiques and designer home accessories. **Via Giulia** and **Via Monserrato** also feature antiques dealers galore, plus a few art galleries. In the **Pantheon** area there are many shops selling liturgical objects and vestments. But the place to go for religious souvenirs is, obviously, the area around

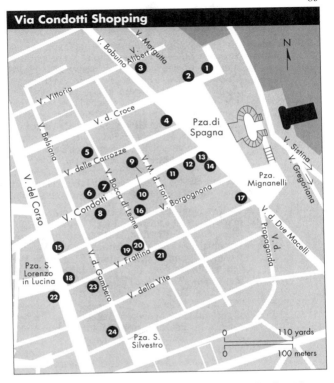

Via Condotti Shopping

Alinari, **3**
Bozart, **19**
Buccellati, **8**
Bulgari, **11**
Camomilla, **4**
Campanile, **6**
Carlo Palazzi, **16**
Di Cori, **17**
Ferragamo, **7, 10**
Fornari, **23**
Frette, **2**

Gucci, **9, 12**
Luisa Spagnoli, **20, 22**
Magli, **24**
Mario Valentino, **18**
Merola, **15**
Miranda, **5**
Myricae, **21**
Roland's, **13**
Sermoneta, **14**
Sorelle Fontane, **1**

St. Peter's, especially **Via della Conciliazione** and **Via di Porta Angelica.**

Department Stores

Rome has only a handful of department stores. **Rinascente,** near Piazza Colonna, sells clothing and accessories only. The Rinascente at Piazza Fiume has the same stock. **Coin,** on Piazzale Appio, near San Giovanni in Laterano, has fashions for men and women. There is another Coin store in the mall at CinecittàDue (*see* Shopping Malls, *below*). The **UPIM** and **Standa** chains offer low to moderately priced goods. They're the place to go for small purchases you need to see you through until you get home. In addition, they carry all kinds of toiletries and first-aid needs. Most Standa and UPIM stores have while-you-wait shoe-repair service counters.

Food and Flea Markets

Rome's biggest and most colorful outdoor food markets are at **Campo dei Fiori** (just south of Piazza Navona), **Via Andrea Doria** (about a quarter mile north of the entrance to the Vatican museums), and **Piazza Vittorio** (just down Via Carlo Alberto from the church of Santa Maria Maggiore). There's a flea market on Sunday morning at **Porta Portese** (on Via Ippolito Nievo, off Viale Trastevere); it now offers mainly new or secondhand clothing, but there are still a few dealers in old furniture and intriguing junk. Bargaining is the rule here, as are pickpockets; beware. All outdoor markets are open from early morning to about 2, except Saturday, when they may stay open all day.

Shopping Malls

The **CinecittàDue** mall was the first of several mega-malls now catering to Roman consumers, and it is the handiest—just take Metro Line A to the Subaugusta stop. The mall has 100 shops, including a **Coin** branch, a big supermarket, snack bars, and cafés (Piazza di Cinecittà, Viale Palmiro Togliatti, tel. 06/722–0902).

Clothing Boutiques

All the big names in Italian fashion—Versace, Ferre, Valentino, Armani, Missoni—are represented in the Piazza di Spagna area. **Sorelle Fontane** (Salita San Sebastianello 6), one of the first houses to put Italy on the fashion map, has a large boutique with an extensive line of ready-to-wear clothing and accessories. **Carlo Palazzi** (Via Borgognona 7) has elegant men's fashions and accessories. **Mariselaine** (Via Condotti 70) is a top-quality women's fashion boutique. **Camomilla** (Piazza di Spagna 85) has trendy styles for women. Bargain hunters will love **Labels-for-Less** (Via Viminale 35), a discount store in the Termini Station vicinity.

Specialty Stores
Antiques and Prints For old prints and antiques, the **Tanca** shop (Salita dei Crescenzi 10, near the Pantheon) is a good hunting ground. Early photographs of Rome from the archives of **Alinari** (Via Aliberti 16/a) make interesting souvenirs. **Nardecchia** (Piazza Navona 25) is reliable for prints.

Handicrafts For pottery, handwoven textiles, and other handicrafts, **Myricae** (Via Frattina 36, with another store at Piazza del Parlamento 38) has a good selection. **La Galleria** (Via della Pelliccia 29) in Trastevere is off the beaten track but well worth a visit; it has a wealth of handicrafts, beautifully displayed in a rustic setting. A bottle of liqueur, jar of marmalade, or bar of chocolate handmade by Cistercian monks in several monasteries in Italy makes an unusual gift to take home; they are all for sale at **Ai Monasteri** (Piazza Cinque Lune 2).

Household Linens and Embroidery **Frette** (Piazza di Spagna 11) is a Roman institution for fabulous trousseaux. **Cesari** (Via Barberini 1 and Via Babuino 195) is another; it also has less-expensive gift items, such as aprons, beach towels, and place mats. **Lavori Artigianali Femminili** (Via Capo le Case 6) offers exquisitely embroidered household linens, infants' and children's clothing, and blouses.

Jewelry **Bulgari** (Via Condotti 10) is to Rome what Cartier is to Paris; the shop's elegant display windows hint at what's beyond the guard at the door. **Buccellati** (Via Condotti 31) is a tradition-rich Florentine jewelry house famous for its silverwork; it ranks with Bulgari. **Fornari** (Via Frattina 71) and **Frugoni** (Via Arenula 83) have tempting selections of small silver objects. **Bozart** (Via Bocca di Leone 4) features dazzling costume jewelry.

Knitwear **Luisa Spagnoli** (Via del Corso 382, with other shops at Via Frattina 116 and Via Veneto 130) is always reliable for good quality at the right price and styles to suit American tastes. **Miranda** (Via Bocca di Leone 28) is a treasure trove of warm jackets, skirts, and shawls, handwoven in gorgeous colors.

Leather Goods **Gucci** (Via Condotti 8 and 77) is the most famous of Rome's leather shops. It has a full assortment of accessories on the first floor; a fashion boutique for men and women and a scarf department on the second floor; and a full complement of Japanese customers, who line up to get in on busy days. **Roland's** (Piazza di Spagna 74) has an extensive stock of good-quality leather fashions and accessories, as well as stylish casual wear in wool and silk. **Ceresa** (Via del Tritone 118) has more reasonably priced fine-leather goods, including many handbags and leather fashions. **Volterra** (Via Barberini 102) is well stocked and offers a wide selection of handbags at moderate prices. **Sermoneta** (Piazza di Spagna 61) shows a varied range of gloves in its windows, and there are many more inside. **Di Cori,** a few steps away, also has a good selection of gloves; there's another Di Cori store at Via Nazionale 183. **Merola** (Via del Corso 143) carries a line of expensive top-quality gloves and scarves.

Nickol's (Via Barberini 21) is in the moderate price range and is one of the few stores in Rome that stocks shoes in American widths. **Ferragamo** (Via Condotti 73) is one of Rome's best stores for fine shoes and leather accessories, and its silk scarves are splendid; you pay for quality here, but you can get great buys during the periodic sales. **Mario Valentino** (Via Frattina 58) is a top name for stylish shoes and leather fashions. **Magli** (Via del Gambero 1 and Via Veneto 70) is known for well-made shoes and matching handbags at high to moderate prices. **Campanile** (Via Condotti 58) has four floors of shoes as well as other leather goods.

Silks and **Galtrucco** (Via del Tritone 18) and **Meconi** (Via
Fabrics Cola di Rienzo 305) have the best selections of world-famous Italian silks and fashion fabrics. You can find some real bargains when remnants *(scampoli)* are on sale.

5 Dining

There was a time when you could predict the clientele and prices of a Roman eating establishment by whether it was called a *ristorante*, a *trattoria*, or an *osteria* (tavern). Now these names are interchangeable. Generally speaking, however, a trattoria is a family-run place, simpler in decor, menu, and service—and slightly less expensive—than a ristorante. A true osteria is a wine shop, very basic and down to earth, where the only function of the food is to keep the customers sober.

As the pace of Roman life quickens, more fast-food outlets are opening, offering tourists a wider choice of light meals. There are variations of the older Italian institutions of the *tavola calda* (hot table) and the *rosticceria* (roast meats), both of which offer hot and cold dishes to be taken out or eaten on the premises, some sold by the portion, others by weight. You usually select your food and pay for it at the cashier, who gives you a stub to give to the counter person when you pick up the food. Newer snack bars are cropping up, and *pizza rustica* outlets selling slices of various kinds of pizza seem to have sprouted on every block.

Despite these changes, many Romans stick to the tradition of having their main meal at lunch, from 1 to 3, although you won't be turned away if hunger strikes shortly after noon. Dinner is served from 8 or 8:30 until about 10:30 or 11. Some restaurants stay open much later, especially in summer, when patrons linger at sidewalk tables to enjoy the cool breeze *(ponentino)*. Almost all restaurants close one day a week (it's usually safest to call ahead to reserve) and for at least two weeks in August, when it can sometimes seem impossible to find sustenance in the deserted city. This is not a bad time to picnic—buy provisions in any *alimentari* (grocery store).

The typical Roman pasta is fettuccine, golden egg noodles that are at their classic best when freshly made and laced with *ragù*, a thick, rich tomato and meat sauce. *Pasta alla carbonara* is usually made with spaghetti or thicker, spaghetti-like *bucatini;* the cooked pasta is tossed with raw egg, chunks of fried *guanciale* (unsmoked bacon), and lots of freshly ground black pepper. *Spaghetti all'amatriciana* has a piquant sauce of tomato, unsmoked bacon, and hot red pepper. Gnocchi, a Roman favorite for Thursday dinner, are tiny dumplings of semolina and potatoes and are served with a tomato sauce and a sprinkling of grated cheese.

Abbacchio, baby lamb, is at its best in the spring; a summer favorite is *pollo coi peperoni*, stewed chicken with peppers. *Fritto misto* usually includes morsels of zucchini, artichokes, and *baccalà* (codfish) fried in batter. *Carciofi*, or artichokes, are served *alla romana*, sautéed whole with garlic and mint, or *alla giudia*, fried whole with each petal crisp and light enough to melt in your mouth. Tender peas are sautéed with prosciutto to make *piselli al prosciutto*.

Local cheeses are mild *caciotta* and sharp pecorino. Fresh ricotta is also used in a number of dishes. Typical wines of Rome are those of the Castelli Romani: Frascati, Colli Albani, Marino, and Velletri.

Tap water is safe everywhere in Rome, so if you're on a budget, order it (*acqua semplice*) rather than mineral water (*acqua minerale*). Expect a bread and cover charge (*pane e coperto*) in all but the simplest places, as well as a service charge (*servizio*) of 10%–15%. A fixed-price tourist menu (*menù turistico*) includes taxes and services, but usually not drinks.

Highly recommended restaurants are indicated by a star ★.

Category	Cost*
$$$$	over 120,000 lire
$$$	65,000–120,000 lire
$$	40,000–65,000 lire
$	under 40,000 lire

*per person for a three-course meal, including house wine and taxes

Central Rome

$$$$
★
Les Etoiles. Memorable is the word for a meal here, both for the food and for the unique, close-up view of the dome of St. Peter's from many tables. The rooftop restaurant of the Atlante Star hotel, adjacent to the Vatican, in the Prati section of Rome, has big window walls to frame the breathtaking view, which is especially magic in the evening when the cupola's graceful curves are illuminated. The menu varies, depending on what the chef chooses at the market. There are interesting pasta dishes with porcini mushrooms or seasonal vegetables, classic or creative risotto (for two), fresh seafood and choice grilled meats. *When you reserve, ask for a table with a view of St. Peter's. Hotel Atlante Star, Via dei Bastioni 1, tel. 06/689-3434, toll-free in Italy 1678-62038. Reservations advised. Jacket and tie preferred. AE, DC, MC, V.*

$$$$ **Le Jardin.** Located in the Parioli residential district, this restaurant is one of Rome's classiest establishments. It's in the exclusive Lord Byron hotel, itself a triumph of studied interior decoration. The imaginative menu is a tempting compendium of seasonal specialties served with style. If they are on the menu, try the risotto with seafood and vegetable sauce or the fillet of beef with morels. *Hotel Lord Byron, Via Giuseppe De Notaris 5, tel. 06/322-0404. Reservations required. Jacket and tie preferred. AE, DC, MC, V. Closed Sun.*

$$$$ **El Toulà.** Take a byway off Piazza Nicosia in Old Rome to find this prestigious restaurant, one of a number in Italy of the same name; all are spin-offs of a renowned restaurant in Treviso in northern Italy. Rome's El Toulà has the warm, welcoming atmosphere of a 19th-century country house, with white walls, antique furniture in dark wood, heavy silver serving dishes, and spectacular arrangements of fruits and flowers. There's a cozy bar off the entrance, where you can sip a *prosecco* (Venetian semi-sparkling white wine), the aperitif best suited to the chef's Venetian specialties, which include risotto with artichokes and *fegato alla veneziana* (liver with onions). *Via della Lupa 29/b, tel. 06/687-3750. Reservations required. Jacket and tie*

required. *AE, DC, MC, V. Closed Sat. lunch, Sun., Aug., Dec. 24–26.*

$$$ **Andrea.** Ernest Hemingway and King Farouk
★ used to eat here; nowadays, you're more likely
to hear the murmured conversation of Italian
powerbrokers. Half a block from Via Veneto,
this restaurant offers classic Italian cooking in
an intimate, clubby setting, in which snowy ta-
ble linens gleam against a discreet background
of dark-green paneling. The menu features such
delicacies as homemade *tagliolini* (thin noodles)
with shrimp and spinach sauce, spaghetti with
seafood and truffles, and mouth-watering
carciofi all'Andrea (artichokes simmered in ol-
ive oil). *Via Sardegna 26, tel. 06/482–1891. Res-
ervations advised. Dress: casual but neat. AE,
DC, MC, V. Closed Sun. and most of Aug.*

$$$ **Da Checcho er Carrettiere.** Tucked away behind
Piazza Trilussa in Trastevere, Da Checcho has
the look of a country inn, with hanging braids of
garlic and an antipasto table that features some
unusual specialties, such as a well-seasoned
mashed potato-and-tomato mixture. Among the
hearty pasta offerings are *spaghetti alla car-
rettiera*, with black pepper, sharp cheese, and
olive oil, and linguine with scampi. Seafood
(which can be expensive) is the main feature on
the menu, but traditional Roman meat dishes
are offered, too. This is a great place to soak up
genuine Trastevere color and hospitality at
prices that are slightly above moderate. *Via
Benedetta 10, tel. 06/581–7018. Reservations
advised. Dress: casual. AE, DC, MC, V. Closed
Sun. dinner, Mon., and Aug. 10–Sept. 10.*

$$$ **Coriolano.** The only tourists who find their way
to this classic restaurant near Porta Pia are like-
ly to be gourmets looking for quintessential Ital-
ian food, and that means light homemade
pastas, choice olive oil, and market-fresh ingre-
dients, especially seafood. The small dining
room is decorated with antiques, and tables are
set with immaculate white linen, sparkling crys-
tal, and silver. Although seafood dishes vary,
tagliolini all'aragosta (thin noodles with lob-
ster sauce) is usually on the menu, as are porcini
mushrooms in season (cooked according to a se-
cret recipe). The wine list is predominantly Ital-
ian, but includes some French and California
wines, too. *Via Ancona 14, tel. 06/855–1122.*

98

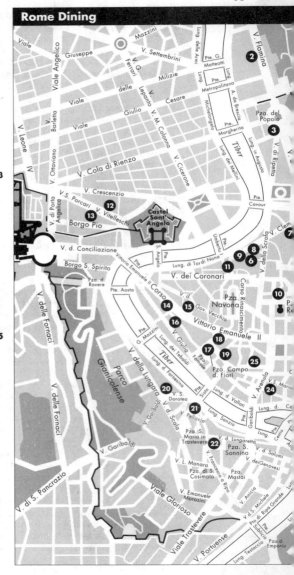

Rome Dining

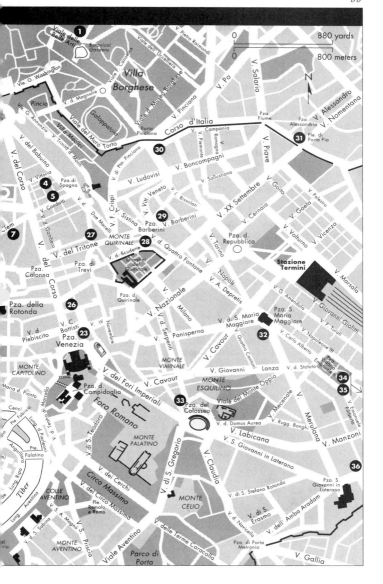

*Reservations advised. Jacket and tie preferred.
AE, DC, MC, V. Closed Sun. and Aug. 1–25.*

$$$ Il Convivio. Don't be intimidated by the opaque
glass, closed door, and doorbell at the entrance.
This, as its name suggests, is a convivial little
restaurant, and it is earning a reputation as one
of Rome's best. Reservations are essential, for it
accommodates only 30 diners. The food is what
it's all about: classic Italian (and Roman) dishes
prepared with flair and a brilliant use of herbs,
as in shellfish with tarragon and lamb with
thyme. The *menù degustazione* (fixed menu) is
good value. *Via dell'Orso 44, tel. 06/686–9432.
Reservations necessary. Dress: casual. AE,
DC, MC, V. Closed Sun.*

$$$ Passetto. Benefiting from a choice location near
Piazza Navona, Passetto has been a favorite
with Italians and tourists for many years: reliable classic Italian food and courteous service.
If you can, eat on the terrace—it's especially
memorable at night; the mirrored dining room is
more staid. Roman specialties, such as *cannel-
loni* (stuffed pasta tubes) and abbacchio, are
featured. *Via Zanardelli 14, tel. 06/654–0569.
Reservations advised. Jacket and tie preferred.
AE, DC, MC, V. Closed Sun., Mon. lunch.*

$$$ Piperno. A favorite, located in the old Jewish
ghetto next to historic Palazzo Cenci, Piperno
has been in business for more than a century. It
is *the* place to go for Rome's extraordinary
carciofi alla giudia (crisp-fried whole arti-
chokes, Jewish-style). You eat in one of three
small wood-paneled dining rooms or at one of a
handful of tables outdoors. Try *filetti di baccalà*
(cod fillet fried in batter), *pasta e ceci* (a thick
soup of pasta tubes and chickpeas), *fiori di
zucca* (stuffed zucchini flowers), and artichokes.
*Monte dei Cenci 9, tel. 06/654–2772. Reserva-
tions advised. Dress: casual. AE, DC, MC, V.
Closed Sun. dinner, Mon., Christmas, Easter,
Aug.*

$$$ Ranieri. Walk down a quiet street off fashiona-
★   ble Via Condotti, near the Spanish Steps, to find
this historic restaurant, founded by a one-time
chef of Queen Victoria. Ranieri remains a favorite with tourists for its traditional atmosphere
and decor, with damask-covered walls, velvet
banquettes, crystal chandeliers, and old paintings. The Italian-French cuisine is excellent:

Portions are abundant, and checks remain comfortably within the lower range in this category. Among the many specialties on the vast menu are *gnocchetti alla parigina* (feather-light dumplings with cheese sauce) and *mignonettes alla Regina Vittoria* (veal with pâté and an eight-cheese sauce). *Via Mario dei Fiori 26, tel. 06/678-6505. Reservations advised. Dress: casual but neat. AE, DC, MC, V. Closed Sun.*

$$ Dal Bolognese. Long a favorite with the art crowd, this classic restaurant on Piazza del Popolo is a handy place for a leisurely lunch between sightseeing and shopping. While dining, feast your eyes on an extensive array of contemporary paintings, many of them by customers, both illustrious and unknown. As the name of the restaurant promises, the cooking here adheres to the hearty tradition of Bologna, with homemade pastas in creamy sauces and steaming trays of boiled meats. For dessert, there's *dolce della mamma*, a concoction of ice cream, zabaglione, and chocolate sauce. *Piazza del Popolo 1, tel. 06/361-1426. Reservations advised. Dress: casual. DC, V. Closed Mon. and Aug. 7-22.*

$$ La Campana. This inconspicuous trattoria off Via della Scrofa has a centuries-old tradition: There has been an inn on this spot since the 15th century, and the two plain dining rooms occupy what were once stables. It's a homey place, with friendly waiters, snowy white linens on close-set tables, and good Roman food at reasonable prices. The menu offers specialties like *vignarola* (sautéed fava beans, peas, and artichokes), rigatoni with prosciutto and tomato sauce, and *olivette di vitello con purée* (tiny veal rolls with mashed potatoes). *Vicolo della Campana 18, tel. 06/686-7820. Dinner reservations advised. Dress: casual. AE, MC, V. Closed Mon. and Aug.*

$$ Cannavota. On the square next to San Giovanni in Laterano, Cannavota has fed generations of neighborhood families. Seafood dominates, but carnivores are catered to, also. Try one of the pastas with seafood sauce—fettuccine with shrimp and scampi is a good choice—and then go on to grilled fish or meat. The cheerful atmosphere and rustic decor make for an authentically Roman experience. *Piazza San Giovanni* *in Laterano 20, tel. 06/772–05007. Reservations advised. Dress: casual. AE, DC, MC, V. Closed Wed. and Aug. 1–20.*

$$ **Colline Emiliane.** Not far from Piazza Barberini is this unassuming trattoria offering exceptionally good food. Behind an opaque glass facade are a couple of plain dining rooms, where you are served light homemade pastas, a special chicken broth, and meats ranging from boiled beef to *giambonetto di vitella* (roast veal) and *cotoletta alla bolognese* (veal cutlet with cheese and tomato sauce). Family run, it's cordial, quiet, and soothing, a good place to rest after a sightseeing stint. *Via degli Avignonesi 22, tel. 06/481–7538. Reservations advised. Dress: casual. No credit cards. Closed Fri. and Aug.*

$$ **Fortunato al Pantheon.** Just a block away from the House of Representatives, Fortunato is a favorite of politicos. (It's also a couple of paces from Piazza della Rotonda by the Pantheon.) With politicians around, there is, of course, a back room, but you can happily settle for the largest of the three dining rooms or even a table outside in good weather. For his faithful and demanding clientele, Fortunato varies his specialties, offering several pastas—such as *penne all'arrabbiata*, with piquant tomato sauce—and *risotto alla milanese*, with saffron, or risotto with porcini mushrooms. He also serves many types of fish and meat dishes, some with expensive truffles. *Via del Pantheon 55, tel. 06/679–2788. Reservations advised. Dress: casual but neat. AE. Closed Sun. and Aug.*

$$ **Le Maschere.** For a taste of southern Italian (Calabrian) fare, look for this cellar restaurant hidden away between Largo Argentina and Piazza Campo dei Fiori. A couple of planters, with a few outdoor tables in summer, mark this informal spot. Downstairs you pass an impressive antipasto buffet, and a pizza oven glows in a corner of the dining room. Dark rustic walls are hung with everything from paper garlands to old utensils; there are pottery wine jugs and rush-bottom chairs. Order spicy Calabria salami to start and then go on to pizza or southern favorites such as pasta with broccoli or with tomato and eggplant sauce. Grilled meat and seafood make up the list of second courses. Music on weekends and efficient service make for a pleasant evening. *Via Monte della Farina 29, tel. 06/ 687–9444. Reservations advised. Dress: casual. AE, DC, MC, V. Dinner only. Closed Mon. and mid-Aug.–mid-Sept.*

$$ Orso 80. This bright and bustling trattoria is located in Old Rome, on a street famed for artisans' workshops. It is known among its local and international followers for a fabulous antipasto table. Try the homemade egg pasta or the *bucatini all'amatriciana* (thin, hollow pasta with tomato sauce and bacon); there's plenty of seafood on the menu, too. For dessert, the ricotta cake, a genuine Roman specialty, is always good. *Via dell'Orso 33, tel. 06/686–4904. Reservations advised. Dress: casual. AE, DC, MC, V. Closed Mon. and Aug. 10–20.*

$$ Osteria da Nerone. Between the Colosseum and the church of San Pietro in Vincoli, this family-run trattoria features a tempting antipasto table and fresh pastas. The specialty is *fettuccine al Nerone* (noodles with peas, salami, and mushrooms), but homemade ravioli are good, too. In fair weather you eat outdoors with a view of the Colosseum. *Via Terme di Tito 96, tel. 06/474–5207. Dinner reservations advised. Dress: casual. No credit cards. Closed Sun. and mid-Aug.*

$$ Otello alla Concordia. The clientele in this popular spot—off a shopping street near Piazza di Spagna—is about evenly divided between tourists and workers from shops and offices in the area. The former like to sit outdoors in the courtyard in any weather; the latter have their regular tables in one of the inside dining rooms. The menu offers classic Roman and Italian dishes, and service is friendly and efficient. Since every tourist in Rome knows about it, and since the regulars won't relinquish their niches, you may have to wait for a table. *Via della Croce 81, tel. 06/678–1454. No reservations. Dress: casual. AE, DC. Closed Sun. and Christmas.*

$$ Paris. On a small square just off Piazza Santa Maria in Trastevere, Paris (named after a former owner, not the city) has a reassuring, understated ambience, without the hokey, folky flamboyance of so many eating places in this gentrified neighborhood. It also has a menu featuring the best of classic Roman cuisine: homemade fettuccine, delicate *fritto misto* (zucchini flowers and artichokes, among other things, fried in batter) and, of course, *baccalà* (fried cod fillets). In fair weather you eat at tables on the little piazza. *Piazza San Callisto 7/a, tel. 06/581–5378. Dinner reservations advised. Dress: casual. AE, DC, MC, V. Closed Sun. dinner, Mon., and 3 weeks in Aug.*

$$ Pierluigi. Pierluigi, in the heart of Old Rome, is a longtime favorite with foreign residents of Rome and Italians in the entertainment field. On busy evenings it's almost impossible to find a table, so reserve well in advance. Seafood dominates (if you want to splurge, try the lobster), but traditional Roman dishes are offered, too, including *orecchiette con broccoli* (ear-shaped pasta with greens) and spaghetti. Eat in the pretty piazza in summer. *Piazza dei Ricci 144, tel. 06/686–8717. Reservations advised. Dress: casual. AE, V. Closed Mon. and 2 weeks in Aug.*

$$ Romolo. Generations of Romans and tourists ★ have enjoyed the romantic garden courtyard and historic dining room of this charming Trastevere haunt, reputedly the one-time home of Raphael's lady love, the Fornarina. In the evening, strolling musicians serenade diners. The cuisine is appropriately Roman; specialties include *mozzarella alla fornarina* (deep-fried mozzarella with ham and anchovies) and *braciolette d'abbacchio scottadito* (grilled baby lamb chops). Alternatively, try one of the new vegetarian pastas featuring *carciofi* (artichokes) or radicchio. Meats are charcoal-grilled; there's also a wood-burning oven. *Via di Porta Settimiana 8, tel. 06/581–8284. Reservations advised. Dress: casual. AE, DC, V. Closed Mon. and Aug. 2–23.*

$$ Tullio. This Tuscan trattoria off Via Veneto and Piazza Barberini opened in the dolce vita days of the 1950s, when this area was the center of Roman chic and bohemian life. It soon acquired a faithful clientele of politicians, journalists, and creative people, and it has changed little over the years. Decor and menu are simple. The latter offers typically Tuscan *pasta e fagioli*, grilled steaks and chops, and *fagioli all'uccelletto* (beans with tomato and sage). *Via San Nicolò da Tolentino 26, tel. 06/481–8564. Reservations advised. Dress: casual but neat. AE, DC, MC, V. Closed Sun. and Aug.*

13

$ **Armando.** One of the best of the many trattorias in this authentic Roman blue-collar district in the shadow of the Vatican, Armando's is a family-run favorite of neighborhood regulars and tourists-in-the-know. The menu offers Roman dishes such as pasta e ceci and *petto alla fornara* (roast veal breast) served with potatoes. *Via degli Ombrellari 41 (at Borgo Vittorio), tel. 06/ 686–1602. Dinner reservations advised. Dress: casual. AE, DC, MC, V. Closed Wed.*

$ **Abruzzi.** Here's a simple trattoria off Piazza Santi Apostoli near Piazza Venezia that specializes in the regional cooking of the mountainous Abruzzo region, southeast of Rome. *Tonnarelli* (square-cut pasta) is served with mushrooms, peas, and ham or with a meat sauce. Abbacchio is another classic regional dish. *Via del Vaccaro 1, tel. 06/679–3897. Lunch reservations advised. Dress: casual. V. Closed Sat. and Aug.*

$ **Baffetto.** The emphasis here is on good old-fashioned value: Baffetto is Rome's best-known inexpensive pizza restaurant, plainly decorated and very popular. You'll probably have to wait in line outside on the cobblestones and then share your table once inside. The interior is mostly given over to the ovens, the tiny cash desk, and the simple, paper-covered tables. *Bruschetta* (toast) and *crostini* (mozzarella toast) are the only variations on the pizza theme. Turnover is fast: This is not the place to linger over your meal. *Via del Governo Vecchio 114, tel. 06/686– 1617. No reservations. Dress: casual. No credit cards. Dinner only. Closed Sun. and Aug.*

$ ★ **Birreria Tempera.** This old-fashioned beer hall is very busy at lunchtime, when it's invaded by businesspeople and students from the Piazza Venezia area. There's a good selection of salads and cold cuts, as well as pasta and daily specials. Bavarian-style specialties such as goulash and wurst and sauerkraut prevail in the evening, when light or dark Italian beer flows freely. *Via San Marcello 19, tel. 06/678–6203. No reservations. Dress: casual, No credit cards. Closed Sun. and Aug.*

$ **Cottini.** For lunch or supper, this cafeteria on the corner of Piazza Santa Maria Maggiore is reliable; the food counter and tables are in the back, beyond the large coffee bar and pastry counters. Salads, hot pastas, and main courses are always fresh, and they are served with a smile. The in-house bakery provides such tempting desserts as crème caramel and chocolate cake. *Via Merulana 287, tel. 06/474–0768. No reservations. Dress: casual. No credit cards. Closed Mon.*

$ Fratelli Menghi. Neighborhood regulars frequent this trattoria that has been in the same family for as long as anyone can remember and produces typical Roman fare. There's usually a thick soup such as minestrone, pasta e ceci, and other standbys, including *involtini* (meat roulades). *Via Flaminia 57, tel. 06/320–0803. No reservations. Dress: casual. No credit cards. Closed Sun.*

$ Grappolo d'Oro. This centrally located trattoria off Campo dei Fiori has been a favorite for decades with locals and foreign residents, one of whom wrote it up in the *New Yorker* some years ago. This measure of notoriety has not induced the graying, courteous owners to change their two half-paneled dining rooms or menu, which features pasta all'amatriciana and scaloppine any way you want them and daily specials. *Piazza della Cancelleria 80, tel. 06/686–4118. Reservations advised. Dress: casual. AE, MC, V. Closed Sun.*

$ Hostaria Farnese. This is a tiny trattoria between Campo dei Fiori and Piazza Farnese, in the heart of Old Rome. Mama cooks; papa serves; and, depending on what they've picked up at the market, you may find rigatoni with tuna and basil, spaghetti with vegetable sauce, *spezzatino* (stew), and other homey specialties. *Via dei Baullari 109, tel. 06/654–1595. Reservations advised. Dress: casual. AE, V. Closed Thurs.*

$ Polese. Come here in good weather, when you can sit outdoors under trees and look out on the charming square off Corso Vittorio Emanuele in Old Rome. Like most centrally located inexpensive eateries in Rome, it is crowded on weekends and weekday evenings in the summer. Straightforward Roman specialties include *fettuccine alla Polese* (with cream and mushrooms) and *vitello alla fornara* (roast brisket of veal with potatoes). *Piazza Sforza Cesarini 40, tel. 06/686–1709. Reservations advised on weekends.*

*Dress: casual. AE, DC, MC, V. Closed Tues.,
15 days in Aug., 15 days in Dec.*

$ **Pollarola.** This typical Roman trattoria, near Pi-
azza Navona and Campo dei Fiori, has flowers
(artificial) on the tables and an ancient, authentic Roman column embedded in the rear wall,
evidence of its historic site. You can eat outdoors
in fair weather. Try a pasta specialty such as *fettuccine al gorgonzola* (egg pasta with creamy
gorgonzola sauce) and a mixed plate from the ar-
ray of fresh antipasti. The house wines are
good. *Piazza della Pollarola 24 (Campo dei
Fiori), tel. 06/6880-1654. Reservations advised
for groups. Dress: casual. AE, V. Closed Sun.*

$ **Tavernetta.** The location between the Trevi
Fountain and the Spanish Steps and the good-
value tourist menu make this a reliable bet for
Sicilian and Abruzzi specialties. Try the pasta
with eggplant or the *porchetta* (roast suckling
pig), and the red or white house wine. *Via del
Nazareno 3, tel. 06/679-3124. Dinner reservations required. Dress: casual. AE, DC, MC, V.
Closed Mon. and Aug.*

Along Via Appia Antica

$$ **L'Archeologia.** In this friendly, intimate farm-
house just beyond the catacombs, you dine in-
doors beside the fireplace in cool weather or in
the garden under age-old vines in the summer.
Specialties include homemade pastas, *abbac-
chio scottadito* (grilled baby lamb chops), and sea-
food. *Via Appia Antica 139, tel. 06/788-0494.
Dinner and weekend reservations advised.
Dress: casual. No credit cards. Closed Thurs.*

$$ **Cecilia Metella.** From the entrance on the Via
Appia Antica, practically opposite the cata-
combs, you walk uphill to a sprawling construction designed for wedding feasts and banquets.
There's a large, vine-shaded terrace for outdoor
dining. Although geared to larger groups, Cecilia Metella gives couples and small groups
good service and fine Roman-style cuisine. The
specialties are the searing-hot *crespelle*
(crêpes), served in individual casseroles, and
pollo alla Nerone (chicken à la Nero; flambéed,
of course). *Via Appia Antica 125, tel. 06/513-
6743. Reservations advised on weekends. Dress:
casual. AE, MC, V. Closed Mon.*

6 Lodging

The wide range of Roman accommodations are graded according to regional standards, from five stars down to one. You can be sure of palatial comfort and service in a five-star establishment, but some of the three-star hotels turn out to be much more modest than expected; they are often superficially spruced up to capitalize on a central location. The old-fashioned Roman pension no longer exists as a category, but, while now graded as inexpensive hotels, some preserve the homey atmosphere that makes visitors prefer them, especially for longer stays.

There are distinct advantages to staying in a hotel within walking distance of the main sights, particularly since much of downtown Rome is closed to daytime traffic. You can leave your car at a garage and explore by foot. One disadvantage, however, can be noise, because the Romans are a voluble people. Ask for an inside room if you are a light sleeper, but don't be disappointed if it faces a dark courtyard.

Because Rome's religious importance makes it a year-round tourist destination, there is never a period when hotels are predictably empty, so you should always try to make reservations, even if only a few days in advance. Always inquire about special low rates, often available in both winter and summer if occupancy is low. Ask for *la tariffa scontata* (the discount rate). If you arrive without reservations, try one of the following **EPT** information offices: Via Parigi 5 (tel. 06/488–3748), Termini Station (tel. 06/487–1270), Leonardo da Vinci Airport (tel. 06/601–1255). All can help with accommodations, free of charge. Avoid official-looking men who approach tourists at Termini Station: They tout for the less desirable hotels around the train station. **CTS,** a student travel agency, can help find rooms; the main office is at Via Genova 16 (10 minutes' walk from the station), tel. 06/46791.

Room rates in Rome are on a par with, or even higher than, those in most other European capitals. Ask whether the rate includes breakfast. An extra charge, anything from 7,000 to 27,000 lire depending on the category of hotel, may be added for this, but remember that you're not obliged to take breakfast in the hotel. If you won't be, make this clear when you check in. Air-conditioning in lower-priced hotels may cost extra; in more expensive hotels it will be included in the price. All hotels have rate cards on the room doors or inside the closet. These specify exactly what you have to pay and detail any extras.

Highly recommended lodgings are indicated by a star ★.

Category	Cost*
$$$$	over 450,000 lire
$$$	300,000–450,000 lire
$$	150,000–300,000 lire
$	under 150,000 lire

All prices are for a standard double room, including tax and service.

$$$$ **Grand.** A 100-year-old establishment of class and style, this hotel caters to an elite international clientele. It's only a few minutes from Via Veneto. Off the richly decorated, split-level main salon—where afternoon tea is served every day—there are a smaller, intimate bar and a buffet restaurant. The spacious bedrooms are decorated in gracious empire style, with smooth fabrics and thick carpets in tones of blue and pale gold. Crystal chandeliers and marble baths add a luxurious note. The Grand also offers one of Italy's most beautiful dining rooms, called simply Le Restaurant. *Via Vittorio Emanuele Orlando 3, tel. 06/4709, fax 06/474–7307. 170 rooms and suites with bath. Facilities: 2 restaurants, bar. AE, DC, MC, V.*

$$$$ **Hassler.** Located at the top of the Spanish Steps, ★ the Hassler boasts sweeping views of Rome from its front rooms and penthouse restaurant; other rooms overlook the gardens of Villa Medici. The hotel is run by the distinguished Wirth family of hoteliers, which assures a cordial atmosphere and magnificent service from the well-trained staff. The public rooms are memorable—especially the first-floor bar, a chic rendezvous, and the glass-roofed lounge, with gold marble walls and a hand-painted tile floor. The

elegant and comfortable guest rooms are decorated in a variety of classic styles, some with frescoed walls. The penthouse suite has a mirrored ceiling in the bedroom and a huge terrace. *Piazza Trinità dei Monti 6, tel. 06/678–2651, fax 06/678–9991. 101 rooms and suites with bath. Facilities: restaurant, bar. AE, MC, V.*

$$$$ Majestic. In the 19th-century tradition of grand hotels, this Via Veneto establishment offers sumptuous furnishings and spacious rooms, with up-to-date accessories such as CNN, minibars, strongboxes, and white marble bathrooms. There are antiques in the public rooms, and the excellent restaurant looks like a Victorian conservatory. *Via Veneto 50, tel. 06/486841, fax 06/488–0984. 95 rooms and suites with bath, many with whirlpool baths. Facilities: restaurant, bar with terrace, garage. AE, DC, MC, V.*

$$$ Albergo del Sole al Pantheon. This small hotel has been opposite the Pantheon since the 15th century. It is tastefully decorated with a blend of modern and antique furnishings. Ceilings are high, floors are terra-cotta tiled, and there is a charming courtyard for al fresco breakfast in good weather. *Piazza della Rotonda 63, tel. 06/678–0441, fax 06/684–0689. 26 rooms with bath. Facilities: bar, nearby garage. AE, DC, MC, V.*

$$$ Farnese. A turn-of-the-century mansion, the
★ Farnese is near the Metro and within walking distance of St. Peter's. Furnished with great attention to detail in art deco style, it has dazzling modern baths and charming fresco decorations. Room rates are low for the category and include a banquet-size breakfast. *Via Alessandro Farnese 30, tel. 06/321–2553, fax 06/321–5129. 24 rooms with bath. Facilities: parking, bar, roof garden. AE, DC, MC, V.*

$$$ Flora. With its Old-World decor and style, now largely refurbished with entirely new bathrooms, the Flora has a solid position among Via Veneto hotels. The rooms are ample, and many have fine views of Villa Borghese. Potted plants bank the public rooms and marble-lined hallways. Period furniture, Oriental rugs, and old paintings add character to the rooms. Attentive service and unostentatious comfort keep regular clientele coming back year after year. *Via Veneto 191, tel. 06/497821, fax 06/482–0359. 175 rooms with bath. AE, DC, MC, V.*

Rome Lodging

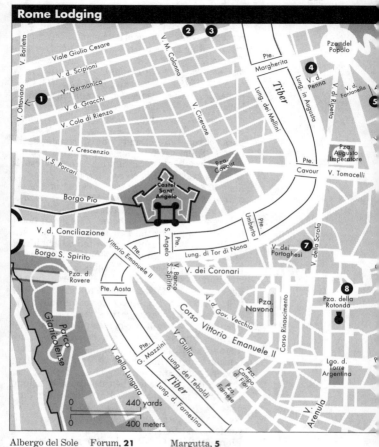

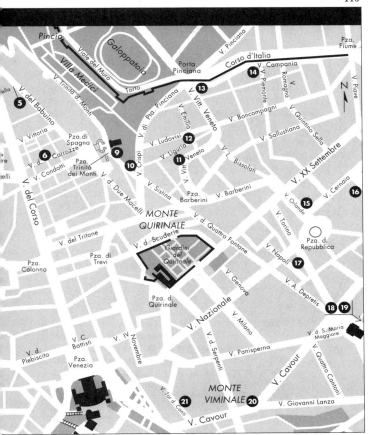

$$$ **Forum.** A centuries-old palace converted into a
★ fine hotel, the Forum is on a quiet street within
shouting distance of the Roman Forum and Piaz-
za Venezia. The wood-paneled lobby and street-
level bar are warm and welcoming. The smallish
bedrooms are furnished in rich pink and beige
fabrics; the bathrooms are ample, with either
tub or shower. What's really special, though, is
the rooftop restaurant and bar, good for a mem-
orable breakfast or nightcap: The view toward
the Colosseum is superb. *Via Tor dei Conti 25,
tel. 06/679–2446, fax 06/678–6479. 76 rooms
with bath. Facilities: restaurant, bar. AE, DC,
MC, V.*

$$$ **Giulio Cesare.** An aristocratic townhouse in the
residential, but central, Prati district, the Giu-
lio Cesare is a 10-minute walk across the Tiber
from Piazza del Popolo. It's beautifully run,
with a friendly staff and a quietly luxurious air.
The rooms have chandeliers, thick rugs, floor-
length drapes, and rich damasks in soft colors.
Public rooms have Oriental carpets, old prints
and paintings, marble fireplaces, and a grand
piano. *Via degli Scipioni 287, tel. 06/321–0751,
fax 06/321–1736. 90 rooms with bath. Facilities:
bar, garden, terrace. AE, DC, MC, V.*

$$$ **Victoria.** Considerable luxury in the public
rooms, solid comfort throughout, and impecca-
ble management are the main features of this
hotel near Via Veneto. Oriental rugs, oil paint-
ings, welcoming armchairs, and fresh flowers
add charm to the public spaces, and the homey
rooms are soothingly decorated in peach, blue,
and green. American businessmen, who prize
the hotel's service and restful atmosphere, are
frequent guests. Some upper rooms and the roof
terrace overlook the majestic pines of Villa Bor-
ghese. *Via Campania 41, tel. 06/473931, fax 06/
487–1890. 110 rooms with bath. Facilities: res-
taurant, bar. AE, DC, MC, V.*

$$ **Britannia.** This small hotel offers superior quali-
★ ty at rates only slightly above moderate prices.
Its quiet but central location and caring man-
agement are attractions: Guests are coddled
with English-language dailies and local weather
reports delivered to their rooms each morning.
Sybaritic marble bathrooms and well-furnished
rooms, especially the decor on the second floor,

where halls are decorated in Pompeiian style, help make this a very special place. *Via Napoli 64, tel. 06/488–3153, fax 06/488–2343. 32 rooms with bath. Facilities: lounge, bar. AE, DC, MC, V.*

$$ Carriage. Stay here for the location, the Old World elegance, and the reasonable rates. The hotel is decorated in soothing tones of blue and pale gold, with subdued Baroque accents; rooms have antique-looking closets and porcelain telephones. Double room 402 and single room 305 have small balconies; room 302 is spacious and elegant, with an oversize bathroom. *Via delle Carrozze 36, tel. 06/699–0124, fax 06/678–8279. 27 rooms and suites with bath. AE, DC, MC, V.*

$$ D'Este. Within hailing distance of Santa Maria Maggiore and close to Termini Station (you can arrange to be picked up there by the hotel car), this is in a distinguished 19th-century building. The fresh-looking decor evokes turn-of-the-century comfort, with brass bedsteads and lamps and dark wood period furniture. Rooms are quiet, light, and spacious; many can accommodate family groups. The attentive owner-manager likes to have fresh flowers in the halls. He encourages inquiries about special rates. *Via Carlo Alberto 4/b, tel. 06/446–5607, fax 06/446–5601. 37 rooms with bath. Facilities: bar, garden terrace. AE, DC, MC, V.*

$$ Duca d'Alba. The Suburra quarter near the Colosseum, where the plebs of ancient Rome lived, is in transition from shabby to chic, and this elegant little hotel comes under the latter heading. Over a refined reception area and small lounge are three floors of compact bedrooms stylishly decorated with light wood and soft colors, with bathrooms in beige travertine. Room rates are low in the category. *Via Leonina 14, tel. 06/484471, fax 06/488–4840. 24 rooms with bath or shower. AE, DC, MC, V.*

$$ Internazionale. With an excellent location near the top of the Spanish Steps, the Internazionale has long been known as one of the city's best mid-size hotels. It has doubly thick windows to ensure peace and quiet. Rooms on the fourth floor have terraces; the fourth-floor suite has a private terrace and a frescoed ceiling. Decor throughout is in soothing pastel tones, with some antique pieces, mirrors, and chandeliers.

Guests relax in small, homey lounges downstairs and begin the day in the pretty breakfast room. *Via Sistina 79, tel. 06/679–3047, fax 06/678–4764. 40 rooms with bath. AE, MC, V.*

$$ Locarno. Off Piazza del Popolo, the Locarno is a favorite among the art crowd, which also goes for its intimate mood, though some of Locarno's fine fin de siècle character has been lost in renovations. An attempt has been made to retain the hotel's original charm, however, while modernizing the rooms with such additions as electronic safes and air-conditioning. The decor features coordinated prints in wallpaper and fabrics, lacquered wrought-iron beds, and some antiques. *Via della Penna 22, tel. 06/361–0841, fax 06/321–5249. 38 rooms with bath. Facilities: bar, lounge. AE, V.*

$$ Portoghesi. In the heart of Old Rome, facing the so-called Monkey Tower, the Portoghesi is a small hotel with considerable atmosphere. From a tiny lobby, an equally tiny elevator takes you to the quiet bedrooms, all decorated with floral prints and reproduction antique furniture. There's a breakfast room. *Via dei Portoghesi 1, tel. 06/686–4231, fax 06/687–6976. 27 rooms with bath or shower. MC, V.*

$$ La Residenza.
★ In a converted town house near Via Veneto, this hotel offers first-class comfort and atmosphere at reasonable rates. The canopied entrance, spacious well-furnished lounges, and the bar and terrace are of the type you would expect in a deluxe category. Rooms, decorated in aquamarine and beige, with bentwood furniture, have large closets, color TV, fridgebar, and air-conditioning; bathrooms have heated towel racks. The clientele is mostly American. Rates include a generous American-style buffet breakfast. *Via Emilia 22, tel. 06/488–0789, fax 06/485721. 27 rooms with bath or shower. Facilities: bar, rooftop terrace, parking. MC, V.*

$ Amalia. Handy to the Vatican and the Cola di Rienzo shopping district, and a block from the Ottaviano stop of Metro Line A, this small former *pensione* is owned and operated by Amalia Consoli and her brothers. On several floors of a 19th-century building, it has 21 newly renovated rooms with TV sets, direct-dial telephones, pictures of angels on the walls, and gleaming marble bathrooms (hair dryers included). The remaining four guest rooms will be redone. *Via Germanico 66, tel. 06/397-23354, fax 06/397-23365. 25 rooms, 21 with bath or shower. Facilities: bar, breakfast room. AE, MC, V.*

$ ★ **Margutta.** This small hotel is on a quiet side street between the Spanish Steps and Piazza del Popolo. Lobby and halls are unassuming, but rooms have a clean and airy look, attractive wrought-iron bedsteads, and modern baths. Though it's in an old building, there is an elevator. *Via Laurina 34, tel. 06/322-3674. 21 rooms with bath or shower. AE, DC, MC, V.*

$ **Romae.** Located in the better part of the Termini Station neighborhood, the Romae has the advantages of a strategic location (within walking distance of many sights and bus and subway lines), a very friendly and helpful management, and good-size rooms that are clean and airy. The vivid pictures of Rome in the small lobby and breakfast room, the luminous white walls and light wood furniture in the bedrooms, and the bright little baths all have a fresh look. Amenities such as satellite TV and a hair dryer in every room, and breakfast included in the room rate, make this hotel a very good value. Families benefit from special rates and services. *Via Palestro 49, tel. 06/446-3554, fax 06/446-3914. 20 rooms with bath. AE, MC, V.*

$ **Montreal.** This is a compact hotel across the square from Santa Maria Maggiore, only three blocks from Termini Station, with bus and subway lines close by. Though on one floor of an older building, it has been totally renovated and offers fresh-looking rooms. The owner/managers are pleasant and helpful, and the neighborhood has plenty of reasonably priced eating places, plus one of Rome's largest outdoor markets. *Via Carlo Alberto 4, tel. 06/446-5522, fax 06/445-7797. 16 rooms with bath or shower. MC, V.*

7 The Arts and Nightlife

The Arts

Rome offers a vast selection of music, dance, opera, and film. Schedules of events are published in daily newspapers; in *Trovaroma*, the weekly entertainment guide published every Thursday as a supplement to the daily *La Repubblica;* in the *Guest in Rome* booklet distributed free at hotel desks; and in the monthly *Carnet*, available free from EPT offices. An English-language periodical, *Wanted in Rome* (1,000 lire), is available at centrally located newsstands and has good listings of events.

Concerts Rome has long hosted a wide variety of classical music concerts, although the city does not have adequate concert halls or a suitable auditorium. Depending on the location, concert tickets can cost from 10,000 to 50,000 lire. The principal concert series are those of the **Accademia di Santa Cecilia** (offices at Via dei Greci, box office tel. 06/678–0743), the **Accademia Filarmonica Romana** (Teatro Olimpico, Via Gentile da Fabriano 17, tel. 06/320–1752), the **Istituzione Universitaria dei Concerti** (San Leone Magno auditorium, Via Bolzano 38, tel. 06/361–0051), and the **RAI** Italian Radio-TV series at Foro Italico (tel. 06/368–65625). There is also the internationally respected **Gonfalone** series, which concentrates on Baroque music (Via del Gonfalone 32, tel. 06/687–5952). The **Associazione Musicale Romana** (tel. 06/656–8441) and **Il Tempietto** (tel. 06/481–4800) organize music festivals and concerts throughout the year. There are also many small concert groups. Many concerts are free, including those in Catholic churches, where a special ruling permits only religious music. Look for posters outside churches announcing free concerts.

Rock, pop, and jazz concerts are frequent, especially in summer, although even performances by big-name stars may not be well advertised. Tickets are usually handled by **Orbis** (Piazza Esquilino 37, tel. 06/482–7403) and **Babilonia** (Via del Corso 185, tel. 06/678–6641).

Opera The opera season runs from November to May, and performances are staged in the **Teatro dell'Opera** (Via Firenze 72, tel. 06/488–1755).

Tickets go on sale two days before a performance, and the box office is open 10–5. Prices range from 26,000 to 142,000 lire for regular performances; they can go much higher for an opening night or an appearance by an internationally acclaimed guest singer. Standards may not always measure up to those set by Milan's fabled La Scala, but most performances are respectable.

The summer opera season has been evicted from the ruins of the ancient **Baths of Caracalla.** At press time it is uncertain where the summer productions will take place. Check locally.

Dance The **Rome Opera Ballet** gives regular performances at the Teatro dell'Opera (*see* Opera, *above*), often with leading international guest stars. Rome is regularly visited by classical ballet companies from Russia, the United States, and Europe; performances are at the Teatro dell'Opera, Teatro Olimpico, or at one of the open-air venues in summer. Small classical and modern dance companies from Italy and abroad give performances in various places; check concert listings for information.

Film Rome has dozens of movie houses, but the only one to show exclusively English-language films is the **Pasquino** (Vicolo del Piede, just off Piazza Santa Maria in Trastevere, tel. 06/580–3622). Films here are shown in English with Italian subtitles. Pick up a weekly schedule at the theater or consult the daily papers.

Nightlife

Although Rome is not one of the world's most exciting cities for nightlife, discos, live-music spots, and quiet late-night bars have proliferated in recent years in the streets of the old city and in far-flung parts of town. The "flavor of the month" factor works here, too, and many places fade into oblivion after a brief moment of popularity. The best up-to-date list of late-night spots is in the weekly entertainment guide *Trovaroma*, a supplement to the Thursday edition of *La Repubblica.*

Bars Rome has a range of bars that have background music. Jacket and tie are in order in the elegant **Blue Bar** of the Hostaria dell'Orso (Via dei Soldati 25, tel. 06/686–4250) and in **Le Bar** of the Grand hotel (Via Vittorio Emanuele Orlando 3, tel. 06/482931). **Jeff Blynn's** (Via Zanardelli 12, tel. 06/686–1990; closed Sun.), near Piazza Navona, is a classic watering hole with seating at the bar or in leather-upholstered booths. Light meals are available. It's open from 7 PM to 2 AM, with happy hour from 7 to 10. **Flann O'Brien** (Via Napoli 29, tel. 06/448–0418; closed Sat. morning and Sun.) has the look and atmosphere of an upscale Irish pub, but it's open all day, also functioning as an Italian coffee bar.

Informal wine bars are popular with Romans who like to stay up late but don't dig disco. Near the Pantheon is **Spiriti** (Via Sant'Eustachio 5, tel. 06/689–2499), which also serves light lunches and is open until 1:30 AM. The same atmosphere prevails at **Enoteca Roffi** (Via della Croce 76/a, tel. 06/679–0896) and at **Cavour 313** (Via Cavour 313, tel. 06/678–5496), near the Roman Forum. All three are closed Sunday. **Trimani Wine Bar,** between Piazza della Repubblica and Porta Pia (Via Cernaia 37/b, tel. 06/446–9630), is the family-run annex of one of Rome's most esteemed wine shops. Sample some great wines at the counter or with a light, fixed-price meal at an upstairs table (open 11:30–3 and 5:30–midnight. Closed Sun.).

"In" places around Piazza Navona and the Pantheon include **Antico Caffè della Pace** (Via della Pace 3, tel. 06/686–1216), and **Le Cornacchie** (Piazza Rondanini 53, tel. 06/686–4485). Both are open until 2 AM.

Beer halls and pubs are popular with young Italians. **Birreria Marconi** (Via di Santa Prassede 9/c, tel. 06/486636; closed Sun.), near Santa Maria Maggiore, is also a pizzeria. **Birreria Santi Apostoli** (Piazza Santi Apostoli 52, tel. 06/678–8285) is open every day until 2 AM. Among the pubs, **Fiddler's Elbow** (Via dell'Olmata 43, no phone; closed Mon.) is open 5 PM–midnight. **Four Green Fields** (Via Costantino Morin 42, off Via della Giuliana, tel. 06/359–5091) features live music and is open daily from 8:30 PM to 1 AM.

Music Clubs Jazz, folk, pop, and Latin music clubs are flourishing in Rome, particularly in the Trastevere neighborhood. Jazz clubs are especially popular, and talented local groups may be joined by visiting musicians from other countries. As admission, many clubs require that you buy a membership card for about 10,000–20,000 lire.

In the Trionfale district near the Vatican, **Alexanderplatz** (Via Ostia 9, tel. 06/372–9398) has both a bar and a restaurant, and nightly programs of jazz and blues played by Italian and foreign musicians. For the best live music, including jazz, blues, African, and rock, go to **Big Mama** (Vicolo San Francesco a Ripa 18, tel. 06/581–2551). There is also a bar and snack food. Latin rhythms are the specialty at **El Charango** (Via di Sant'Onofrio 28, tel. 06/687–9908), near Ponte Amedeo d'Aosta, a live music club.

In the trendy Testaccio neighborhood, **Caffè Latino** (Via di Monte Testaccio 96, tel. 06/574–4020) attracts a thirtysomething crowd with concerts (mainly jazz) and a separate video room and bar for socializing. **Music Inn** (Largo dei Fiorentini 3, tel. 06/654–4934; closed Mon.–Wed.) is Rome's top jazz club and features some of the biggest names on the international scene.

Live performances of jazz, soul, and funk by leading musicians draw celebrities to **St. Louis Music City** (Via del Cardello 13/a, tel. 06/474–5076; closed Thurs.). There is also a restaurant.

Discos and Most discos open about 10:30 PM and charge an
Nightclubs entrance fee of around 30,000–35,000 lire, which may include the first drink. Subsequent drinks cost about 10,000–15,000 lire. Some discos also open on Saturday and Sunday afternoons for under-16s.

There's deafening disco music at **Frankie-Go** (Via Schiaparelli 29–30, tel. 06/322–1251; closed Mon.) for the under-30 crowd, which sometimes includes young actors. Special events, such as beauty pageants and theme parties, are featured, and there is a restaurant. The entrance is on Via Luciani 52.

Jackie O' (Via Boncompagni 11, tel. 06/488–5754) is a favorite with the rich and famous for dinner and/or disco dancing. Roman yuppies mingle with a trendy and sophisticated crowd while dancing to disco music at **Spago** (Via di Monte Testaccio, tel. 06/574–4999; it's hard to find, so take a taxi). **Fonclea** (Via Crescenzio 82/a, tel. 06/689–6302), near Castel Sant'Angelo, has a pub atmosphere, Mexican and Italian food, and live music ranging from jazz to Latin American, depending on who's in town.

Go to **Gilda** (Via Mario dei Fiori 97, near Piazza di Spagna, tel. 06/678–4838; closed Mon.) to spot famous Italian actors and politicians. Formerly the Paradise supper club, this hot nightspot now has a new piano bar, as well as a restaurant, dance floors, and live music. **Hysteria** (Via Giovanelli 12, tel. 06/855–4587; closed Mon.) attracts a very young crowd who come to enjoy the disco, funk, soul, and hard rock. It's located off Via Salaria near the Galleria Borghese. A glittering disco, piano bar, and restaurant attracts over-25s to the **Open Gate** (Via San Nicola da Tolentino 4, tel. 06/474–6301). Dancing starts at midnight.

One of Rome's first discos, **The Piper** (Via Tagliamento 9, tel. 06/841–4459; closed Mon. and Tues.) is an "in" spot for teenagers—disco music, live groups, and pop videos. Occasionally, there's ballroom dancing for an older crowd. It opens weekends at 4 PM. Funky music and huge video screens make **Scarabocchio** (Piazza Ponziani 8, tel. 06/580–0495; closed Mon.) another popular spot.

Follia (Via Ovidio 17, tel. 06/683–08435) attracts celebrities and a sophisticated young crowd with disco music and a piano bar.

For Singles Locals and foreigners of all ages gather at cafés on **Piazza della Rotonda** in front of the Pantheon, at **Piazza Navona**, or **Piazza Santa Maria in Trastevere**. The cafés on **Via Veneto** and the big hotel bars are good places to meet travelers in the over-30 age group. In fair weather, under-30s will find crowds of contemporaries on the **Spanish Steps**.

Index

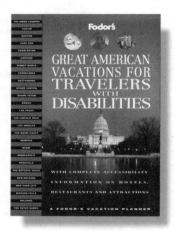